SIX ARMENIAN POETS

SIX ARMENIAN POETS

Translated by Arminé Tamrazian
Edited and introduced by
Razmik Davoyan

2013

Published by Arc Publications
Nanholme Mill, Shaw Wood Road
Todmorden, OL14 6DA, UK
www.arcpublications.co.uk

Copyright in the poems © individual poets as named, 2013
Copyright in the translation © Arminé Tamrazian, 2013
Copyright in the Introduction © Razmik Davoyan, 2013

Design by Tony Ward
Printed in Great Britain by
TJ International, Padstow, Cornwall

ISBN: 978 1906570 87 3

The publishers are grateful to the authors
and, in the case of previously published works,
to their publishers for allowing their poems
to be included in this anthology.

Cover image: Minas Avetisyan

This book is copyright. Subject to statutory exception and to
provisions of relevant collective licensing agreements,
no reproduction of any part may take place without the
written permission of Arc Publications Ltd.

The pubishers are grateful to the
Armenian Ministry of Culture
for their unstinting help in the preparation of this volume.

The 'New Voices from Europe and Beyond' anthology series
is published in co-operation with Literature Across Frontiers
which receives support from the Culture programme of the EU.

LITERATURE
ACROSS
FRONTIERS

**Arc Publications 'New Voices from Europe and Beyond'
Series Editor: Alexandra Büchler**

CONTENTS

Series editor's preface / 9
Introduction / 11

HRACHYA SARUKHAN
Biography / 19

20 / "Անձրեւի կաթիլ…" • "A raindrop…" / 21
20 / "Մի անգամ…" • "Once…" / 21
22 / Աշնանային Անավարտ Տողեր • Unfinished Autumnal Lines / 23
30 / "Իմ ձայնից այն կողմ ամայություն էր…" • "There was nothing beyond my voice…" / 31
30 / Եվ Քանի Որ… • And Since… / 31
32 / Տպավորություն • Impression / 33
32 / "Երազամուտ Կանխածայն…" • "A Call to Enter a Dream…" / 33

VIOLET GRIGORIAN
Biography / 39

40 / Էլեգիա • Elegy / 41
42 / 1993թ • 1993 / 43
44 / "Սեւ օրվա պահուստ ցոլցուն զինիʹ…" • "Sparkling wine saved for a dark hour…" / 45
46 / Մահվան Հարսնացուն • Death's Betrothed / 47

KHACHIK MANOUKYAN
Biography / 55

56 / " Անիծված են…" • "Cursed are…" / 57
56 / Անցյալ • Past / 57
58 / Անապատ • Desert / 59
58 / Գիշերային Էսքիզ • Nocturnal Sketch / 59
60 / "Խեղճ ու կրակ մի մոմ…" • "A meagre lone candle…" / 61
62 / "Մեզ որոնեցի ալիքների մեջʹ…" • "I searched for you in the waves…" / 63
62 / Վիրավոր Խաչ • A Wounded Cross / 63

AZNIV SAHAKYAN
Biography / 71

72 / "Գարունը ձայրից ձայր…" • "Spring is pulsating blue…" / 73
72 / "Երգում են ծաղիկները…" • "The flowers are singing…" / 73
74 / "Սիրտս ծամում էիʹ փափկացնելու համար…" • "I was chewing on my heart to soften it…" / 75
74 / "Սենյակիս անդունդը մեծանում է…" • "The abyss in my room is growing deeper…" / 75

76 / "Կարմիր է դողը ջրերի…"	"The quiver of the water is red…" / 77
76 / "Աշունն իջնում էր…"	"Autumn was descending…" / 77
78 / "Մութը ստվերն է ձայնիս…"	"Darkness is the shadow of my voice…" / 79
78 / "Խուլ է պգրուկը գիշերվա…"	"Deaf is the leech of the night…" / 79
78 / "Տերևներ՝ ուշացող անձրևների մասին խոսող…"	"Leaves, telling of delayed rains…" / 79
80 / "Տողերի թռչունները սև…"	"The black birds of the lines…" / 81
80 / "Ես քար եմ երևի…"	"Perhaps I am stone…" / 81
80 / "Բառերը լապտերներ են փնտրում…"	"The words are seeking torches…" / 81
82 / "Ծառերի նման, որ ծաղկում ու թավիվում են սիրուն…"	"Like a tree, which blossoms and thins nicely…" / 83
82 / "Ձների մեջ սրտիս…"	"In the snows of my heart…" / 83
84 / "Լուսինն ազդագրի նման կախվեց փողոցի վրա՛…"	"The moon hung over the street like a billboard…" / 85

ANATOLI HOVHANNISYAN
Biography / 89

90 / "Ես ինձ փնտրում եմ…"	"I seek myself…" / 91
90 / "Բանաստեղծության տող՝…"	"A line of poetry…" / 91
90 / "Օրացույցի մեջ կորած մի օր…"	"A lost day on the calendar…" / 91
90 / "Քամին մռխիրը համբուրելով…"	"The wind has burnt its lips…" / 91
92 / "Քնած ես…"	"You are asleep…" / 93
92 / "Ես կորչում եմ քո նվազ աչքերում…"	"I am lost in your fainting eyes…" / 93
92 / "Ես ասպղերի արտացոլանքը…"	"I'm a breathless river…" / 93
92 / "Մենակ են ծառերը…"	"The trees are alone…" / 93
94 / "Դատարկությունը լցվում է վախի ճիչով…"	"Emptiness is filled with screams of fear…" / 95
94 / "Ես եմ, ինչ ունես այս կյանքում…"	"I am all you have in life…" / 95
96 / "Ես ինքս իմ մեջ խճճված…"	"I'm a fishing net…" / 97
96 / "Ես կրկնում եմ անունս…"	"I keep repeating my name…" / 97
96 / "Ես ապրում եմ սպասման մեջ…"	"I live in anticipation…" / 97

98 / "Մենակ եմ…" • "I am alone…" / 99
98 / "Գեղանկարի • "Torn pieces of a
պատառոտված կտորներ…" painting…" / 99
100 / "Փոշի…" • "Dust…" / 101
100 / "Լուսմութին ձյունը…" • "The snow sleeps in the twilight…" / 101
102 / Երբ Վերքը Դառնում Է • When the Wound Turns into
Կոշտուկ a Callus / 103
102 / "Մայրուղուն դաջված…" • "Flattened on the motorway…" / 103
104 / "Խառը երազների • "I have woken…" / 105
շփոթից…"

HASMIK SIMONIAN
Biography / 109
110 / "Ճերմակ լռության • "In the solace of a white
սփոփանքի մեջ…" silence…" / 111
112 / բարև • Hello / 113
114 / "Օրերը ծխախոտներ էին • "Days were smoking
ծխում…" cigarettes…" / 115
116 / մերրիին • To Mary / 117
120 / "ակորդեոնի պես • "Among the autumns which
բացվող-փակվող աշունների stretched and squeezed like
միջից…" an accordion…" / 121

About the Editor & Translator / 125

SERIES EDITOR'S PREFACE

Six Armenian Poets is the tenth volume in a series of bilingual anthologies which brings contemporary poetry from around Europe to English-language readers. It is not by accident that the tired old phrase about poetry being 'lost in translation' came out of an English-speaking environment, out of a tradition that has always felt remarkably uneasy about translation – of contemporary works, if not the classics. Yet poetry can be and *is* 'found' in translation; in fact, any good translation *reinvents* the poetry of the original, and we should always be aware that any translation is the outcome of a dialogue between two cultures, languages and different poetic sensibilities, between collective as well as individual imaginations, conducted by two voices, that of the poet and of the translator, and joined by a third interlocutor in the process of reading.

And it is this dialogue that is so important to writers in countries and regions where translation has always been an integral part of the literary environment and has played a role in the development of local literary tradition and poetics. Writing without reading poetry from many different traditions would be unthinkable for the poets in the anthologies of this series, many of whom are accomplished translators who consider poetry in translation to be part of their own literary background and an important source of inspiration.

While the series 'New Voices from Europe and Beyond' aims to keep a finger on the pulse of the here-and-now of international poetry by presenting the work of a small number of contemporary poets, each collection, edited by a guest editor, has its own focus and rationale for the selection of the poets and poems.

In *Six Armenian Poets*, we are introduced to the poetical memory of a nation steeped in folklore and myth, combined with a determination to forge new ideas through writing. Despite widespread censorship during the period of Soviet rule, Armenia's poets and readers continued to look for inspiration in the glimpses they caught of Western modernism and of their own pre-Soviet poetry. It is in this search that their dissidence manifested itself, and it is in the enduring search to combine the old with the new that these six poets show us the vigour of their nation's contemporary poetry. As Razmik Davoyan suggests in his introduction, we can read in their work the opening up of the Armenian psyche to a fascinating new, global awareness.

I would like to thank all those who have made this edition possible.

Alexandra Büchler

INTRODUCTION   / 11

We can see where Armenian poetry comes from simply by looking at the fragments of our pre-Christian epic stories recorded by the fifth-century historian Movses Khorenatsi in his *History of the Armenians*. The events depicted in those stories go back to primaeval times, long, long before this last civilization, perhaps even to the birth of mankind. Those stories reached Khorenatsi through oral tradition and, by recording them, he presented our nation with an invaluable gift.

The roots of the Armenian ancient epic stories reach back to the beginnings of mankind. "Tsovinar" (daughter of the seas), the mother of our nation and goddess of the waters, conceived her two sons "Sanasar" and "Baghdasar" from the waters. The most ancient memories of this nation relate them to "Sis" and "Masis" (the small and large peaks of Mount Ararat respectively). What processes were at work on our planet at the time when these two saintly brothers ("Sanasar" means Sacred Mountain) were born is for the oceanographers, astronomers and scientists to determine... However, at a later period, life continued on earth thanks to Sanasar, who held Noah's Ark on his shoulders. Tsovinar existed when the Lord's eye (or spirit) roamed over the dark waters, earth, sky and land when the waters had not yet separated. The animals, even before Adam and Eve, had not yet been created. Tsovinar, herself illuminated as the very waters by the Lord's Spirit, gave birth to everything else. Water is the beginning of everything and Tsovinar, the goddess of the waters, has never disappeared from our memories. Furthermore, in an epic poem of the early middle ages called 'The Brave Men of Sassoon', it is Tsovinar who provides the warriors with their mythical flaming swords and flying horses to withstand the Arab invasions.

In short, our poetical memory goes far beyond our historical memory. In fact, our primary history is our poetry, which should be considered as being totally free from falsehoods, offering a sincere and impartial account because it was not commissioned by any ruler or princely house. In this poetical history, "Vahagn" (the god of war, courage and victory in Armenian mythology) is also born from the seas.

> The sky was in labour,
> The earth was in labour
> And the golden sea was in labour
> And within the sea
> The red reed was in labour.
> Smoke rose from the reed stem,
> Flames rose from the reed stem

> And through the flames there ran
> A young adolescent.
> He had hair of fire on his head,
> A beard of flames
> And his eyes were suns.

The storytellers of the early middle ages would sing 'The Birth of Vahagn' to the accompaniment of a cithara (or lyre), telling of how he fought devils, lightning and evil forces and Khorenatsi wrote these stories down. During later periods, the characters in these epic stories have appeared and reappeared constantly in different folk tales, fables, and narratives.

The bed-rock of Armenian poetry is a strong and revered folklore tradition that has produced many outstanding poets from the middle ages to modern times, both in Eastern and Western Armenia.

During the Soviet era, most of these writers were banned authors. At the same time, for the writers of a nation deprived of its roots, everything beyond the Iron Curtain was shrouded in mystery; because ideas were being created in nations free from state control, they had an attractive and rather tempting lustre and assumed a dream-like desirability. Western modernism was "crushed" by Soviet critics in articles and literary criticism whose mission was to glorify social realism, but with the passing years it became more and more obvious for the artists and writers that this was only a result of ideological corruption and had no artistic or aesthetic value whatsoever. The "crushers" themselves, however, were also fully aware of this fact; therefore, especially during the post-Stalin years, quotations from authors representing bourgeois and modernist ideologies took up a substantial part of their works. Needless to say, these long quotations were intended for the benefit of those who were searching tirelessly to get a glimpse of the ongoing ideological processes in the outside world. In other words, there seemed to be a secret pact between the critics and the writers which sometimes resembled a game, as in the story of Adam and Eve in the Bible, where God brings the forbidden fruit to their attention by forbidding them to taste it. Naturally they eventually did taste it and their minds were opened.

After Stalin's death another, more touching, internal pact was formed between poets and readers. Although Khrushchev had denounced the worship of the individual, overall policy had remained unchanged as he himself notes in his Memoirs. Khrushchev admits that he and his administration blindly believed and trusted in Stalin's idea of creating one "Soviet Nation" from over seventy ethnic groups and nations living within the boundaries of the empire and it was this preposterous idea that led the Communist Party and its strong censorship to suppress even the weakest manifestation – in any form whatsoever – of national sentiment. The level of oppression varied in different republics. For instance, in the Ukraine in the city of Lvov, during a festival dedicated to Armenian literature in 1973, the present writer was forbidden to read a poem on national television, despite the fact that it had already been published in Russian translation in Moscow. At the same time, the persecutions and prosecutions of poets making public speeches were reduced considerably. Audiences applauded excitedly whenever a poet gave them a positive, or even a vague, idea of freedom or national sentiment from the stage. There was a covert pact between poet and audience which was a source of the most powerful vital energy both for the poet and the people. It was during this period that, having undergone the necessary censorships, writers of the past began to be re-published. Queues at bookshops for pre-Soviet literature and desirable books by contemporary writers were common, provoking envy and hatred from writers in the service of the Party, who now used their position to block the way – at all costs – for the truly talented writers. In spite of all this, those were comparatively heart-warming years as it seemed that our nation's book-worshipping tradition was being revived. However, Western modernism still continued to tempt young writers in Armenia, which unfortunately proved to be a very poor option, perhaps due to the fact that the so-called "modernists" followed the writers of the Soviet Baltic republics, considering them closer to the West. Illegal literature was passed from hand to hand, the style and substance of which ranged from trash to that worth emulating.

There was no "samizdat" in Armenia. This was either because of the small size of the Republic and tight state control, or perhaps because Armenian writers simply did not create such works. There was, however, dissidence. It is possible that the entire nation was defiant; everyone was passively seeking new political and social freedoms. Those few who questioned, however discreetly, the underlying structures immediately found themselves under surveillance by the security services.

It should be mentioned here that dissidence does not belong to literature. Dissidence belongs to politics and the highest literary values reject it. It is common knowledge that ruling powers always try to use the people's heroes or heroines for their own ends. Every state or regime has, to a differing degree, its share of crimes against humanity, human rights and freedom. It is also common knowledge that a true artist will always stand up for freedom, human rights and humanity, and is always with, and part of, the people. If a true poet is defiant, his defiance rises beyond the reach of politics on the wings of his poetry which thus remains relatively untouched.

In post-Khrushchev Soviet Armenia, it often happened that the henchmen of the Writers' Union and their serving critics denounced the works of brilliant writers as "anti-Soviet and nationalistic" in order to strengthen their position before their ruling lords on the one hand, and on the other, to provide satisfaction and a sense of victory over true talent for their obliging mediocrity. There were certainly pressures and persecutions but fortunately they did not result in death or exile as was common practice in earlier times.

In Soviet Armenia, irrespective of the substance, the classical form of poetry was most commonly used and although the writer familiar with our literary heritage would know that historically, perfect specimens of many different forms of poetry exist in Armenian literature. Speaking personally, I do not have a preference towards any particular form, because for me poetry, as with any other art form, is a means of conveying life energy from the creator to the "consumer". In the same way that electricity is conveyed from its source through the wire to the lamp at the other end which turns it into light, the life energy should be conveyed from the creator through their creation to the reader's (or listener's or viewer's) perfect heart and turned into light (of a poem, an image or a piece of music). The reader, then, is free to make a choice and whether the form is classical or free, or whether there is a sequence of varying forms, the requirement is always the same. The words should be linked together to perfection in order to be able to convey both life energy and what the poet has to say simultaneously. The rest, that is the amount of life energy which each creator has to give, is determined only by Providence.

Three of the poets included in this volume, Hrachya Saroukhan, Azniv Sahakyan and Khachik Manoukyan, established themselves as poets in the post-Stalin Soviet Armenia. Violet Grigorian and Anatoli Hovhannisyan are partly from the Soviet era, although they have become more visible since the independence. The youngest, Hasmik Simonian, is a post-Soviet writer.

There is a considerable amount of affection directed towards HRACHYA SAROUKHAN, perhaps because of the fact that, having studied in the capital city Yerevan, he established himself as a poet without moving from his home in the country, even though his talent did give him the right to demand his place in the city. From his small town, having gained the affection of the readers in his own environment, he managed to establish himself with the literary public as one of the finest representatives of his generation. By drawing his friends, relatives and his very loyal followers into his poems, Saroukhan creates an interpersonal poetic environment in which, using various tricks, he weaves pictures in micro-strokes of their confessions, memories, or sometimes their thorn-crowned losses, throwing a not-very-confident glance at the other world.

On the other hand, KHACHIK MANOUKYAN candidly announces his credo, "This Isn't The World", the title of his latest collection of poems. The starting point of his struggle against the inhuman nature of this world is the scriptures, the Old and New Testaments. He complains to Noah, arguing that perhaps he didn't choose the right people with which to start the new, faithful humankind, and that, as a result of his misjudgment, the world today is ruled by brutish regimes and laws. It is in this struggle that we find Manoukyan's true vitality both as a person and as a poet.

VIOLET GRIGORIAN and HASMIK SIMONIAN belong to different generations but, with a united philosophy, they have no fear of endangering the "poetry" in favour of the consolation of creating something from the ruins of their inner worlds caused by the cruelty of life. Their attempts to break free from interpersonal and domestic inconveniences prompt them to use certain linguistic tools with which they are able to "bring out the domestic trash" and indulge in an involuntary psychological distortion. Armenia's closed, traditional lifestyle has been opened up, and these two poets fearlessly intend to use their right to uncontrolled freedom of speech to the very end. In other words, preserving the "poetry" in their creations is not their prime concern. Whether this is right or wrong is for the reader to judge.

The other two poets represented in this volume also "dig up" their poems from the exploration of their inner feelings, but with one crucial difference. They try as much as they possibly can not to compromise the "poetry".

AZNIV SAHAKYAN has entitled her latest collection of poems *Back Door*, providing the reader with a hint as to the way into the treasury of her inner world, while at the same time making it clear that the social creature which people can see only represents the physical picture of her distorted existence. In this selection, the reader can become acquainted with Sahakyan's sombre existence. Her visual system of self-expression is truly attractive and in harmony with her psychological state.

ANATOLI HOVHANNISYAN's collection of poems, *Mirror*, is not a smooth, single-surfaced mirror, but rather consists of many fragments, each of which reflects an invaluable relic of agonizing feelings which eventually form a uniform poetic world that cannot leave the sensitive reader untouched. This mirror is not meant to reflect the image of the author or the reader, and those who seek this will be disappointed. In the mirror of suffering, each reader can find a fragment of their own suffering and it is these fragments that come together to form the poet's own mirror. Anatoli Hovhannisyan does not aim to cause suffering to the reader by his own torment. Rather, he brings about a feeling of consolation, whether intentionally or not, which could be considered a mirror of solace.

Razmik Davoyan

HRACHYA SARUKHAN

HRACHYA SARUKHAN was born in 1947 in Armenia. In 1963 he entered the Terlemezyan State School of Fine Arts and in 1970 he began studying literature at Vanadzor Institute of Pedagogy. He has worked as a teacher, as Head of the literature and philosophy sections of the Institute of Pedagogy, and as Head of the literature section of H. Abelyan Theatre. He has also worked as a journalist.

In 1990 he was elected secretary of the Vanadzor division of the Writers' Union of Armenia. A member of the Writers' Union of the Soviet Union, he spent two years in Moscow following a two-year post-graduate course at the M. Gorky Institute of Literature. He has published the following collections: *Finishing Lines* (1977), for which he received the Best First Book of the Year award; *Magical Days* (1981); *Testimonies* (1989), for which he was awarded the Av. Isahakyan prize; *Other Times* (1997); *God's Morning* (1999); *Plus* (2005); and *Wreath of Love* (2005). He was awarded the Annual Prize of the Writers' Union of Armenia in 1997 and in 1998 he received the Movses Khorenatsi medal from the President of the Republic of Armenia.

* * *

Անձրևի կաթիլ.
Էլի՛ մի կաթիլ.
Միևնույն տեղում –
Մի երրո՛րդ կաթիլ...

Խելագարվո՛ւմ եմ
Անձրևի նման,
Անձրևի նման –
Կաթիլ առ կաթիլ:

* * *

Մի անգամ,
Երբ մուրացկաններին
3ույց տվի ոսկեդրամներս,
Նրանք կուրացան:
Երբ ասացի՝
Ձեր հարստությունն է սա,
Վերցրե՛ք և բուժեք ձեր աչքերը,
Նրանք խլացան:
Հետո,
Ոսկեդրամների փոխարեն,
Նրանք գրոշներ վերցրին ուրիշներից
Եվ իրենց հորինած հեքիաթներում
Փորձեցին
Թուղթ պեզասներով
Նրանց հասցնել Պառնաս...

* * *

A raindrop
Another raindrop
On the very same spot
A third raindrop...

I'm going mad
Like the rain
Like the rain –
Drop by drop.

* * *

Once
I showed the beggars
My gold coins
And they were blinded.
When I said –
These are your treasures
Take them and heal your eyes –
They were deafened.
Instead,
They took copper from others
And in the tales they made up
Tried to raise them to Parnassus
On the wings of a paper Pegasus...

ԱՇՆԱՆԱՅԻՆ ԱՆԱՎԱՐՏ ՏՈՂԵՐ

1

Կարմիր փերևները
Սեւանում են խոնավ փողոցների վրա։
Իրիկնային մութը աստղե գավաթներով
Դատարկել է փողծում սիրտը ջրհորների,
Եվ գետերի ճիչը քարանում է մի պահ
Ջրհորների խոնավ աչքերի մեջ։
Իսկ սրճավրան ծխում օդը սրճահամ է
Ու քայլերիս նման երերուն է մի քիչ։
Իսկ աչքերս իրենց խիստ տկար են զգում
Լապտերների դժգույն շուրջպարի մեջ...
Կարմիր փերևները
Սեւանում են խոնավ փողոցների վրա,
Եվ հուշերիս արկղը թափանցիկ է դառնում,
Եվ տեսնում եմ ահա դեմքը նրա։

2

Ու նրա հետ
Ահա
Ես մփնում եմ այգի.
Նափարաններ, ես ձեզ չեմ մոռացել
Եվ հիշում եմ, ծառեր, ձեր զգեստը հանվող։
Եվ թռիչքն եմ հիշում ես ջրերի
Համաչափ ու ընդհատ շատրվանվող,
Եվ կարոտիս ճիչն եմ լսում ահա
Մեղապարտի մոլոր զգուշությամբ...
Մենք քայլում ենք խաղաղ,
Մենք չենք խոսում ոչինչ,
Եվ երեկոն սեր է մեզ խոստանում,
Եվ բռնում է
Ձեռքս ձեռքի վարանումը,
Եվ ժպտում է նա ինձ ու խոստանում։

UNFINISHED AUTUMNAL LINES

1

The red leaves
Turn black on the damp pavements.
The darkness of the evening tries to empty
The sorrow of the wells with star bowls
And the scream of the rivers is frozen for an instant
In the wet eyes of the wells.
And the air in the café, stirring like my faltering steps,
Smells of coffee.
And my eyes feel weary
In the wan dance of the torches…
The red leaves
Turn black on the damp pavements,
And my box of memories becomes transparent,
I can now see her face.

2

And so I enter the park
With her.
Benches, I haven't forgotten you
And trees, I recall your thinning garb.
And I recall the fountains of water
Shooting up at regular intervals
And I hear the scream of my longings
With the uncertain caution of a sinner…
We walk in peace
We talk of nothing
And the evening promises love
And my hand
Holds the doubt in hers
And she smiles at me and hesitates.

3

Ինքնասպանները սպանում են մահին
Ու երկինք են գնում խաղաղությամբ,

Իսկ դու,
Ինքնասպան դու իմ կարո՛ր,
Սպանեցիր դու քեզ։
Իսկ ես
Դեռ ապրում եմ,
Իսկ նա
Ապրում է դեռ,
Դեռ սերը կա։
Նույն աչքերն են էլի – թեեւ սեւով ներկած,
Նույն շուրթերը – հիմա համբույրների կծիկ,
Բայց որքան էլ կյանքը դաշույն ցցի
Չի մնալու սերն իմ այսպես ընկած...

Իսկ դու,
Ինքնասպան դու իմ կարո՛ր,
Սպանեցիր դու քեզ։

4

Իմ սենյակը ճերմակ լույս է սիրում,
Մինչդեռ շաղախվել է լույսը քո աչյունով,
Եվ մոխրագույն լույս է շուրջս փիրում։
Իսկ ես, չիմանալով մոխրագույնի լեզուն,
Ամբողջովին վատ եմ հասկանում ինձ։
Իսկ ես, չիմանալով մոխրագույնի քայլը,
Չեմ հասկանում ո՛ւր եմ ես տանում ինձ։
Իսկ սերը կա...

3

Suicides kill death
And go to heaven in peace,

And you,
The one I yearn for,
You murdered yourself.
And I
Still live
And she
Still lives
Love still is.
Still the same eyes – though painted black
The same lips – now a tangled ball of kisses,
But no matter how many wounds life inflicts
My love won't remain fallen…

And you
The one I yearn for,
You murdered yourself.

4

My room is full of light
But the light is suffused with your memory,
And around me all is grey.
And I, not knowing the language of grey,
Don't understand myself at all.
And, being unfamiliar with the footsteps of grey,
I don't know where I'm going.
Yet love is…

5

Արտասուքով,
Միայն արտասուքով
Ես կարող եմ հիշել փողն առաջին –
Անքնության ձեռքով մի օր գրված։
Իսկ սենյակում՝
Հիմա
Ձեռագրեր գրված,
Իսկ սենյակում՝
Հիմա
Տողերի կույտ...

Աշու՛ն,
Դու անցյալ ես,
Դու կորուստ ես դեղին։
Քո մռացված դեմքը նարինջ է մի
Իմ հուշերի դատարկ արկղում պահվող,
Եվ իմ անքնության հորանջն ես դու,
Տերևներից քամվող մահերգի մեջ...

Արտասուքով,
Միայն արտասուքով
Ես կարող եմ հիշել փողն առաջին՝
Անքնության ձեռքով մի օր գրված։

6

Ու ես
Դեռ ապրում եմ,
Ու նա
Ապրում է դեռ,
Դեռ սերը կա։
Եվ կա գիրքը,
Որ դողացող ձեռքի խորհուրդն ունի իր մեջ –
Չվերձանվող սիրո ինքնագրով։
Ու ես դեռ չեմ այրել ոչ մի նամակ՝
Ջիմանալով, որ ես կջերմանամ։
Ու ես դեռ ապրում եմ...
Իսկ ինչո՞ւ եմ ապրում,
Չէ՞ որ ինքնասպանը սպանում է մահին,
Իսկ իմ մահը արդեն... քսան տարեկան է։

5

With tears,
Only with tears
Can I recall the very first line
Penned by the hand of sleeplessness one day.
And in the room
Now
Scattered manuscripts,
And in the room
Now
A pile of lines…

Autumn
You are history
You are a yellow void.
Your forgotten face is an orange
Held in the empty box of my memories,
And you are the yawn of my sleeplessness,
An elegy squeezed from the leaves…

With tears,
Only with tears
Can I recall the very first line
Penned by the hand of sleeplessness one day.

6

And I
Still live
And she
Still lives
Love still is.
And the book still is –
Which is worth a hand trembling
With the undecipherable autograph of love.
And I still haven't burnt any letters
Without knowing that I'll be warmed by them.
And I still live…
And why do I live?
Does the suicide not murder death?
Yet my death is now… at twenty.

7

Եվ նստել եմ ահա,
Եվ ծխում եմ նորից ես իմ գլանակը:
Իմ դիմացի պատից մի նկար է նայում
Աստվածամոր գլխի թեք շարժումով,
Եվ իմ հիշողության պատառների վրա
Իր համբույրը թողած հեռանում է Հուդան:

Ես գրքեր եմ հիշում նկարազարդ,
Եվ այդ նկարներից
Նույն Հիսուսն է նայում՝
Մերթ թշնամի որպես,
Մերթ հարազատ...

Աշու՛ն,
Դու անցյալ ես,
Դու կորուստ ես դեղին
Եվ իմ լինելության պատկերն ես բարդ,
Ու ես այսուհետեւ
Ինձ մատնիչ եմ զգում
Եվ զգում եմ ես ինձ –
Աստվածամարդ...

8

Գլանակս հալվեց իր ծխի մեջ
Եվ իր մոխիրներում գտավ իր հանգիստը,
Իսկ ես –
Տագնապում եմ,
Իսկ ես –
Անհանգիստ եմ...

Իսկ թերթերում
Էլի մահազդեր են փվում,
Եվ փվում են նոթեր ճամփորդական,
Եվ գրքեր են էլի գրվում անթիվ –
Պլատոնյան սիրո ընբռնումով...

7

I'm sitting now
Smoking my fag again.
From the wall opposite a picture is looking at me
With a kindly glance from the Virgin
And Judas makes off having left his kiss
On the canvas of my memories.

I remember illustrated books
And Jesus himself looking at me
From those pictures
At times as an enemy,
At times as a brother...

Autumn, you are history
You are a yellow yearning
And the complex picture of my existence.
Henceforth,
I'll feel myself a traitor
I'll feel myself –
A creation of God...

8

My fag was consumed in its own smoke
And found peace in its ashes
But I
Am troubled
But I
Am worried...

And in the papers
Obituaries are still published
And travel notes are still published
And countless books are still written
With the understanding of platonic love...

* * *

Իմ ծայնից այն կողմ ամայություն էր,
Բորբոսնած երկինք ու որդնած ձյուն էր...
Գիշերը կույր էր, առավոտը՝ խուլ,
Ցերեկը՝ համար, երեկոն՝ խարխուլ...

Գնա՛մ, ժողովեմ մոխիրը ծայնիս,
Փրկեմ բառերիս աճյունափոշին,
Գլուխս դնեմ մամռոտ մի քարի
Ու արցունք թափեմ թվերում մոշի։

ԵՎ ՔԱՆԻ ՈՐ...

Անհեթեթ բան է
Սրճարանում ձխի օղակներ թողնելը։
Անհեթեթ է
Մայթին ընկած ժանգոտած դանակը հացի։
Բանաստեղծի կողցրած կոպեկները
Գրոշ չարժեն
Կույր մուրացկանների համար։
Անհեթեթ է նաեւ
Չորացած հասկերի զառանցանքը...

Երկնքում
Միշտ էլ աստղեր կլինեն,
Լուսնի լույսը
Կհամբուրի շուրթերը ձյան,
Եվ քանի որ երբեք չի թարգմանվի
Համրերի
Արվեստը քերթության,
Ինչ-որ տեղ
Իր հերթական փուլը կապրի
Անհեթեթ պապերազմը։

* * *

There was nothing beyond my voice
A stale sky and worm-infested snow...
The night was blind and the morning deaf
The day was mute and everything frail...

It's time to gather the ashes of my voice,
Save the remains of my words,
Rest my head on a mossy stone
And weep in the blackberry bush.

AND SINCE...

It is a worthless thing
To leave smoke rings in the café.
The rusty bread-knife thrown on the pavement
Is a worthless thing.
The coins lost by the poet
Aren't worth a penny
To the blind beggar.
The ravings of the dried-up ears of wheat
Are worthless...

There will always be
Stars in the sky,
The moonlight will kiss
The lips of the snow.
And since
The mute's use of words will never be deciphered,
A worthless war,
Somewhere,
Will run its
Usual course.

ՏՊԱՎՈՐՈՒԹՅՈՒՆ

Ծառերի խոնավ բարձրությունը
գածր էր
բառերի ալեգորիկ սահանքից:
Երեխաս հեռու էր,
եւ լացը շատ էր անբնական:

Թաց խոտերից
վաղահաս սիրո հոտ էր գալիս,
գեխաջուրն անցնող շունը
նման էր կասկածամիտ իմաստունի,
եւ անթափանց պատկերի շուրջը
չփորձարկված զենքի փայլ էր կաթում:

(Տերեւների փոսիկներում ծվարած
խարխափող թռչունների երամ):

Օրվա այդ պահը թերեւս փխրուր չլիներ,
եթե մենավոր անցորդի աչքերում
արցունքներ երեւային:

   * * *

Երազամուտ Կանխասածյն:
Նոյի անվան Ջրիեղեդ:
Ե՛ս եմ եղել Ագռավն այն:
Աղավնին ե՛ս եմ եղել:

Կես Աղավնի, կես Ագռավ, –
Դեգերում եմ մինչ այսօր:
Հնար չկա՛ դառնամ կով –
Ինքըս իմ մեջ պակասող:

Մերթ՝ ձիթենու ճյուղի հետ,
Մերթ՝ ջրահեղձ դիերի...
Հնար չեղավ՝ դառնամ եւ –
Ամբողջական, անթերի...

IMPRESSION

The height of the tall, damp trees
Was lower
Than the allegoric flight of weeping words.
The child was far away
And its cry most unnatural.

The wet grass
Smelt of premature love,
The dog passing through the mud
Resembled a suspicious wise man
And around the impenetrable pictures
There dripped the glow of untested weapons.

(A flock of birds
Was hiding among the leaves.)

That very moment of the day
Could perhaps have not been so poignant
Had there been tears
In the eyes of the passer-by.

* * *

A call to enter a dream.
A flood by the name of Noah.
I used to be the raven.
I used to be the dove.

Half-raven, half-dove
I am wandering to this day,
Shrinking within myself
Unable to turn into clay.

Now with an olive branch,
Now with the drowned bodies…
Unable to return home
As a whole, undamaged…

Մինչդեռ, Լյառրն իմ նախնյաց,
Կանխածայն եմ լսում ես...
Բիբլիական դուռդ բա՛ց,
Նոյի նման մտնեմ ներս:

I hear the call
From the mountain of my forbears…
Open up your biblical doors for me
To enter as Noah did.

VIOLET GRIGORIAN

PHOTO: AUTHOR'S ARCHIVE

VIOLET GRIGORIAN, poet and essayist, was born in 1962 in Tehran before her family moved to Armenia in 1976. One of the founders of the literary journal *Inqnagir*, she currently serves as its editor.

The author of five books of poems, Grigorian has won the Writers' Union of Armenia Poetry Award for *True, I'm Telling the Truth* (1991), and the Golden Cane Prize in literature for *The City* (1998). Her poems have been anthologized in France, and in the English-language collections *Anthology of the Armenian PEN Centre* (Yerevan, 1999); *From Ararat to Angeltown* by Emily Artinian, (London, 2005); *The Other Voice: Armenian Women's Poetry Through the Ages* (2006); and *Deviation: an Anthology of Contemporary Armenian Literature* (2008). Her poems have also been translated into Slovak, Macedonia, Georgian and Ukrainian.

ԷԼԵԳԻԱ

Աշնան թափուր վանդակում
դեղին վերեւներ՝ արնոտ, ցանուցիր,
արնոտ փետուրներ- ահա եւ ողջը,
հրեղեն հավքին կապուն կերել է:

Եվ անվերադարձ կորավ ամեն ինչ...

Ճերմակ ձեռնոցներ՝ սպեղնաշարին,
եւ դաշնամուրի սեւ փայլի վրա
թիսկարմիր վարդ՝ թանձր, մոլեգին.
նուրբ մատիկներն են վարժ ելեւէջում,
եւ մեղեդին է ելնում հարցմունքի.
      Համե՞ղ էր բուրը հրեղեն հավքի:
      Համեղ էր, համեղ, – սեւ կապուների
ժիր երգչախումբն է քառաձայն բիսկում:

Եվ անվերադարձ կորավ ամեն ինչ...

Կապույտ շղարշներ՝ ըմբոստ-նվագուն,
եւ պարուհին է ձիգ, շնորհալի
շղարշների մեջ կայծկլտում-մարում,
մերթ սլանում է, հանկարծ ընկրկում
ու պփփվում է ոտքի մատներին, ո'նց է պտտվում,
եւ' արալեզ է, եւ' հոգեհմա,
մեռյալ փետուրներն է ոգեկոչում...
      Կերված բդերը, ավա՜ղ չեն հառնում, –
զիլ կապուների կոշտ երգչախումբն է գուժկան զկրտում:

Եվ անվերադարձ կորավ ամեն ինչ...

Էլ չի հնչելու երգը կախարդիչ,
եւ չի ծաղկելու
եւ չի ծաղկելու
եւ չի ծաղկելու այլեւս երբեք
չորացած այգին.
Նայի՛ր, փշրվեց փետուրը վերջին,
Նայի՛ր, պարուհին ինքն իր պտույտում մարեց, չքացավ,
եւ վերջին վարդն է, նայի՛ր մոլեգին
անդունդի վրա ճօճվում գլխիվայր...

ELEGY

Yellow leaves in the empty cage of autumn
blood-stained, scattered
blood-stained feathers – that's all,
the cat has eaten the firebird.

And everything is lost forever...

White gloves on the keyboard,
And on the black sheen of the piano
A dark red rose, thick, fierce.
Delicate fingers move skillfully
And the tune rises to question
    Was the leg of firebird good?
    Good it was, good the choir
of the black cats belches in four-part harmony.

And everything is lost forever...

blue tulle, wild-weak,
and the dancer, gifted, slim
sparkles and fades in the tulle,
now she soars, now retreats,
turns on tiptoe – and how she turns.
Life giving and enchanting,
she calls upon the dead feathers...
    – the devoured legs, alas, won't rise –
The full chorus of the high pitched cats hiccups the message of doom.

And everything is lost forever...

The enchanting song shall never be heard,
The withered orchard
Shall never blossom,
Shall never blossom, ever again.
Look, the last feather in pieces,
Look, the dancer faded, disappeared in her own twirls,
And the last rose – see –
Is fiercely hanging head down, over the gorge...

Աշնան վանդակում՝ կրծած ոսկորներ...
ահա եւ ողջը – կրծած ոսկորներ...

Եվ անվերադարձ կորավ ամեն ինչ...
Եվ անվերադարձ կորավ ամեն ինչ...

1993Թ-

Այս ինչ դժվար ձմեռ է, սեր իմ, մանրամասն, բշիշ առ բշիշ ինձ սիրիր,
փոքրիկ ու հարմար քարանձավ գտիր ինձ համար,
զարդարիր չքնաղ, այլաշխարհիկ իրերով,
կավե ու փայտե ամաններդով, փափուկ գորգերով, նախշուն կարպետներով,
պտաք ու սիրուն շորեր առ ինձ համար,
թարմ, արևակաթ միս բեր, խորովիր,
ու կուտենք միասին, բերանուներս լիքը կիսսենք,
ու ոչ մի բառ չի հասկացվի, ու կծիծաղենք,
ու յուղը կծորա դնչերիս...
ու երջանիկ, երջանիկ կլինենք:

Գուցե սա իմ վերջին ձմեռն է,
գուցե չեմ տեսնելու՝ ինչպես են ծաղկելու ծառերը ա՛յս անգամ,
իսկ ծաղկելու՜ են նրանք, սեր իմ, ծաղկելու՛ են արդյոք...
Ինձ սիրիր, ինչպես օտար, հեռու երկինքների տակ սիրում են կանանց,
ախ, տեսնե՜ս, ինչպե՛ս են սիրում
ծովեզրյա աղաբույր քաղաքում, հյուսիսի սառց կղզիներում
կամ հառավում՜ կիզիչ արևի, անձանոթ բույսերի,
պտաք համեմունքների, գույնզգույն փետուրներով թռչունների աշխարհում:

Ինձ սիրիր, ինչպես Փարիզում կամ Եգիպտոսում՛
շբեղորեն ազատ, հաճելի ծույությամբ,
կամ ինչպես շաղրայով պարսկուհուն Թեհրանում հիմա – մոլեգին խանդով,
կամ՛ ճապոներեն սիրո բառեր շշնջա իմ ականջին...

Գուցե սա իմ վերջին ձմեռն է,
գուցե չեմ տեսնելու՝ ինչպես են չվաց թռչունները վերադառնալու,
իսկ վերադառնալու՜ են նրանք, սեր իմ, վերադառնալու՛ են արդյոք...
Ու թե ուզենաս, քեզ համար աղջիկ կծնեմ՛ մեկ-երկու ամսում,
ես դա կարող եմ,
իմ միջից նա կելնի, ինչպես որ նավը ներ ծովախորշից,

There are chewed-up bones in the autumn cage...
That's all – the chewed-up bones...

And everything is lost forever...
And everything is lost forever...

1993

It's such a harsh winter, my love, love me in detail, cell by cell,
Find me a small cosy cave,
Adorn it with delightful, other-worldly things,
With pots of clay and wood, soft rugs, colourful carpets,
Get me warm, pretty clothes,
Bring me fresh, juicy meat, grill it for me
And we shall eat and talk with full mouths
Unable to make out a word of what we say, then we'll laugh
And dripping will trickle down our chins...
And happy, happy we shall be.

Perhaps this is my last winter,
I won't see trees blossom again,
But will they, my love? Will they blossom...?
Love me as women are loved under foreign, far-away skies,
Oh, I wonder how they are loved
In the salt-scented town by the sea, in the frozen islands of the north,
Or in the south, the land of the scorching sun, of unknown plants,
Of hot spices, of bright-feathered birds.

Love me as if in Paris or Egypt,
Magnificently free, with a pleasant languor,
Or like the veiled Persian woman in Tehran now – with a fierce jealousy
Or whisper into my ear, love words in Japanese...

Perhaps this is my last winter,
I won't see migrant birds return,
But will they, my love? Will they return...?
And if you wish, I'll bear a girl for you in a month or two,
I can, you know,
She will rise from me as a ship from a narrow bay

ու կլողա դեպի քեզ, դեպի քո սիրո բաց ծովերը,
գույնզգույն փետուրներով մի աղջիկ, այլաշխարհիկ պտուղ,
թխամորթ մի եգիպտուհի, որ հանկարծ կրկլյա ճապոներեն, սեր իմ,
ու երջանիկ, երջանիկ կլինենք։

Իմ սիրիր, կերակրիր եւ փաբացրու,
որ չսափկեմ այս ձմեռ,
ու թե չսափկեմ, սեր իմ, վեսնելու եմ՝
ինչպես են ծաղկելու ծառերը այս անգամ,
ու թե ինչպես են վերադառնալու
(ես գիփեմ, չեռ վերադառնայու են)
գույնզգույն թռչունները՝ փեսնելու եմ, սեր իմ,
ու հենց որ լսեմ ծլվլոցն առաջին,
թողնելու եմ քեզ, սեր իմ, եւ աղջկաս, եւ քարանձավս
ու գնալու եմ հեռու՛, հեռու՛,
չես պահի, սեր իմ, մեկ է, գնալու եմ...

   * * *

Մեռ օրվա պահուստ ցոյցյուն զինի՛,
արի քեզ խմեմ,
ինչ էլ որ լինի
սրանից սեռ օր էլ չի լինելու։

Բայց այս ովքե՞ր են շուրջս խլվլում,
ոչ հորս կողմից են բարեկամ, ոչ մորս,
բայց ինձ հարազատ քույրիկ են ասում
եւ նման են ինձ աչքերի թվով։

Պղպոր պանդոկի ծախու ուրուներ,
մոպ եկեք, նսփեք,
հնձված խոպերի հիշատակն հարցենք։
(Երանի շարքով, էդ խոպերի պես,
վե՛ր կանգնեինք քո փան դռան առջեւ,
էդ խոպերի պես իրար հավասար...
էլ չջոկեիր, ներս թողնեիր մեզ)։

Վհատ թռչուններ,
պատիվ ունեցա ձեզ ճանաչելու,

And will swim towards you, your open seas of love,
A girl with bright feathers, an other-worldly fruit,
A dark-skinned Egyptian, who will suddenly tweet in Japanese, my love,
And happy, happy we shall be.

Love me, feed me and keep me warm
So I survive this winter
And if I do, my love, I shall see
The trees blossom
And the migrant birds return
(I know they will return)
I shall see the colourful birds, my love,
And once I hear the very first chirp
I shall leave you, my love, and my daughter and my cave
To go far, far away,
You won't keep me, my love, I'll go anyway…

* * *

Sparkling wine saved for a dark hour
come, let's drink you up
no matter what,
the hour can't get any darker.

But who are the people fiddling about,
related neither to mother nor to father
but who say they are truly my sisters
and are like me in that they have the same number of eyes?

Ghosts of a murky guesthouse
come closer, sit down,
let's pay our respects to the mowed grass.
(Lord, I wish we could stand in rows
by your door like the grass,
equal like grass shoots…
then you wouldn't choose, but let us all in).

Despairing birds
I had the honour of knowing you,

ինչապիսի՞ն լինեմ,
որ դուք ինձ հարգեք:
Ինչապիսի՞ն լինեմ, ի՞նչ շորեր հագնեմ,
ի՞նչ բառեր ասեմ եւ որպե՞ռ կանգնեմ:

Գուցե կանաչ զլխարկ դնեմ
ու վազվզե՞մ մի ծառի շուրջ,
գուցե կանգնեմ օպերայի խաչմերուկում,
կարգավորե՞մ երթեւեկը քամիների,
գուցե գնամ էս խլնքոտ տղաներից
պապահածի՞ն մարմնս տամ նարնջագույն,
գուցե բիկամ խատրուտիկնե՞ր,
վիշեմ-հանձնեմ քամիներին,
գուցե խմեմ էնքան մինչեւ դառնամ խադո՞դ, ծառի վերեւ՛,
խոտի ցողու՞ն, ջրի կաթի՞լ, ծփի բմբու՞լ...

Փողս այրծավ,
իզուր չրնկնեմ էլ դեսուդեն,
էս մի շիշն էլ պարտքով վերցնեմ
ու փուն գնամ,
քնարեր հաբ կուլ տամ մի բուռ,
գրկեմ շիշն ու՛
ուղի՞ղ... դրախտ:
Կեսգիշերին
նոր, թեւավոր ընկերներիս հետ կխմեմ:

Եղբայրներ իմ, որ ինձ նման
ունեք երկու աչք ու մի քիթ,
թույլ չտաք, որ Կիմա՛ն հիշի մի շիշ գինին
ու եսմահու ինձ անիծի:
Պարտքս փակեք:

ՄԱՀՎԱՆ ՀԱՐՄՆԱՑՈՒՆ

Եվ ի՞նչ լռություն-
  բյուր հազար ձկներ խորքում ջրերի
  բերանիկները բացուխուփ արին,
Եվ ի՞նչ քնքշություն-
  բյուր հազար թավշե ալ ժապավեններ

what should I do
for you ever to respect me?
What should I do? what should I wear?
what should I say? where should I stand?

Perhaps I should wear a green hat
and run around a tree,
perhaps I should stand at the Opera junction
controlling the traffic of winds,
perhaps I should give the snotty boy
my orange body,
perhaps I should belch up bubbles
Then throw them away to the winds,
perhaps I should keep drinking until I turn into grapes, a leaf,
a grass shoot, a drop of water, a bird's feather…

My money's all gone,
let's not wander about any longer,
better borrow this one bottle
and go straight home,
swallow a handful of sleeping pills,
hold the bottle tight and
straight… to heaven.
By midnight
I'll be drinking with my new winged friends.

Brothers, who like me have two eyes and a nose,
don't let Kima think much about the bottle of wine
and curse me posthumously.
Do pay off my debt.

DEATH'S BETROTHED

And such dead silence –
   in the depths of the waters many thousands of fish
   opened and closed their tiny mouths,
And such tender grace –
   many thousands of red velvet ribbons

երկնքից առկախ ծածանվեցին մեղմ,
Եվ ի՞նչ պայծառ բիր-
    բյուր հազար հավքեր գաղտ փետուրները
    կոպիս քսեցին, քունքիս հպեցին կտուցները փափ,
Ի՞նչ փոխակերպում-
    բյուր հազար ծաղիկ հոտոտեցին ինձ
    և փվեցին ինձ նոր կարգավիճակ արքայավարդի,
Ի՞նչ թսան բանակ-
    բյուր հազար փդա՝ ծուռվից ու մերժված,
    փսփինքները կախ սովդաքար դարձան,
Ի՞նչ ճոխ հարսանիք-
    բյուր հազար խոճկոր մսիկներն իրենց
    խոհարարների դափին հանձնեցին,
Ի՞նչ խնամիներ՝ պչրասեր, կոկիկ-
    բյուր հազար գաւտիկ կրցքին շարվեցին
    թթթիկ քամու ու պասդացրին պուտիկները սև,
Ի՞նչ փևական կիրք-
    բյուր հազար դերձակ հարսական շորիս
    բյուր հազար մանրիկ կոճակներ կարեց - դանդաղ բանալի,
Ի՞նչ բազմապատիկ ինքնամատուցում-
    բյուր հազար ճարտար մոգ ու ածպարար
    սև գլխարկներից դուրս բերեցին ինձ,
    ու ես ժպտացի բյուրհազարապատիկ
    քեզ, իմ փեսացու,

Եվ ի՞նչ փեսացու, ախ, ի՞նչ փեսացու, ինչ ջոջ թագավոր, ինչ ճարսվիկ որսկան, հմուտ ձկնկուլ և ժիր սիրեկան, ինչ անվրեպ կի և ինչ կիրթ հարված, ազդտի մեկնող, խաշակիր նավազ, վերջին բարեկամ, վերջին փարփածու, ախ, ի՞նչ փեսացու...
    Նա ինձ կտրանի գիրթ կեռմաններով՝ դեպ արքայությունն իր ապաշխարհիկ, նա իմ սև կառքը ճոխ կզարդարի գիպսե ոսկեզօծ հրեշտակներով, մեփաղե սառը վարդերով ապա, ինչ անց կկացնի մազե կամուրջով և նեղ դոներով բանդագուշանքի, ինձ կառաջնորդի կամարի փակով հկա փողոկրի՝ մինչն արխիվներն իր հիշողության, և կոմպյուտերային աչոք անսխալ ինձ կցուցանի հակիրճ դրվագներ բորոդ անցյալիս... Օ՛, չիք վերադարձ:
    Եվ բանադրված իր ադուփներով նա ինձ կուղեկցի մացտ առ մացտ՝ դեպի ջրերը իր անթափանցիկ, դեպ մոռացություն...
Եվ վերջին անգամ վերջին անունս գր՛նգ կգրնգա – դատարկ սափորում կենտ ավազհատիկ, հպանցիկ հնչյուն, բեկուն անդրադարձ... Ինձ կպարկեցնի ջրերի վրա՝ հյուսկեն դագաղում

    hang from the sky above, fluttering slightly,
And such a bright eye –
    many thousands of birds touched my eyelids
    with their gold feathers, and my temples with their warm beaks,
Such transformation –
    many thousands of flowers sniffed me
    to give me a new status as a peony,
Such a lousy army –
    many thousands of boys, dim and rejected
    turned into snotty-nosed merchants,
Such a lavish wedding –
    many thousands of piglets
    offered their meat to the judgment of the cooks,
Such in-laws – prim, proper,
    many thousands of ladybirds lined up on the bosom
    of the frisky wind and made their black dots sparkle,
Such lasting passion –
    many thousands of dressmakers sewed
    many thousands of tiny buttons onto my dress – slow to undo,
Such manifold self-presentation
    many thousands of magicians
    retrieved me from their black hats
    and I smiled a thousand-fold
    at you, my groom,

And such a groom! Oh, what a groom! A lord and king, avid hunter, skilful heron, vigorous lover, accurate cue and refined strike, ace of diamonds, crusader knight, very last friend and last lover. Oh, what a groom...

He will take me through winding roads to his unworldly kingdom, adorn my black coach with golden angels made of plaster, then with cold, metal roses will take me across the bridge of hair and through the narrow doors of ravings will lead me through the huge ivory arch to the archives of his mind, and with the accurate eyes of a computer will show me brisk episodes of my sick past... Oh, there's no return.

And cursed with his wasteland, he will guide me, bush by bush, towards his turbid waters, towards oblivion... And ding-dong! My latest name will chime for the last time – in the empty urn a single grain of sand, a trivial note, distorted reflection... He will lay me upon the waters, in a coffin woven from seaweed and

զրիմուռների, ու կիամբուրի հոդ առ հոդ նրբին ու ինձ կորորի փրփուրի շրթին - ճերմակ քողերով մեծ արքայավարդ՝ նախկին Վիոլետ, նախկին... չեմ հիշում, այլևս անվարք, ուստի՝ անբասիր, ուստի՝ հրեշտակ, ուստի պղպջակ...

Եվ հար հարաճուն այդ պարապուտում լոկ կոմպյուտերային բիբը փեսանող դեռ կգրանցի պատկերը վերջին իր հիշողության գաղտնադարանում — բյուր հազար թավշե ժապավենների հեղձուկ քնքշանքում՝ ոսկեթեփուկ ձուկ (դեռ թպրտացող, դեռ թպրտացող, դեռ թպրտացող)...

will kiss me tenderly, joint by joint and will rock me on the lips of the foam – a large peony with white veils, former Violet, former... I can't recall, already without guile, therefore chaste, therefore an angel, therefore a bubble...

And in that ever-expanding emptiness, only the all-seeing eye of the computer will still register the last picture – in the stifling grace of many thousands of velvet ribbons a golden-scaled fish (still floundering, still floundering, still floundering)...

KHACHIK MANOUKYAN

KHACHIK MANOUKYAN was born in 1964 in Echmiatzin and in 1989 he graduated from the Yerevan Polytechnic Institute. He has been a member of the Armenian Writers' Union since 1991, and has won numerous awards including the state 'Golden Reed' prize.

His published collections include *My Garden* (1987), *A Wounded Cross* (1992), *An Amazing Time* (1992), *Survival Feast* (1996), *Layer* (1998), *Biblical Intervals* (2001), *Ara and Semiramis* (2002), *Minus, Plus and the others* (2003), *Bypasses* (2004), *Documentations* (2008), *Gold-feathered Mist* (2009), and *Not the World We Know* (2010).

He has been translated into English, French, German, Russian and Farsi.

* * *

Անիծված են՝
Սիրտը,
Բա՛նը,
Հոգի՛ն:
Համակարգիչ, հրթիռ ու մեքենա
Եվ ծայրագույն ուրիշ բաներ խրթին
Հերթով շոշափելով՝ անցիր-գնա:

Կարոտներիդ դեղնած հավաքածուն
Փոքր քամու թեփին –
դժո՛խք ու մա՛հ,
Մեղադափայլ կյանքի սպորացում –
Տեսիլքներից ոչինչ էլ չմնաց:

Մնաց սերը գերված –
փուչ հղացում
Կամ ապառիկ վրվող խայտանք ջրիկ:
 – Մակընթացով խուժած իրարանցում,
 Այս անհովիվ հոտը քոնն է լրիվ:

ԱՆՑՅԱԼ

Այսպեղ չկա ժամանակ՝
Գիշեր է կամ առավոտ,
Մի ձիավարս գլանակ
Մերկանում է հուշի մոտ:

Կարճահասակ մի ծերուկ
Ծիծաղում է ու լալիս,
Նա բռնել է փոքրիկ ձուկ,
Որ նվիրի թշվառիս:

Բայց ինձ ինչու՞ է թվում,
Թե ծերուկը փուն չունի,
Նրան երկինքն է թովում
Առաստաղը գնչուի:

***

Cursed are
The heart,
The word,
The soul.
Computers, missiles, machines
And other extreme, complex stuff –
Pass them by touching each.

Spread your wilted bundle of yearnings
Upon the wings of the wind –
              hell and death,
Humiliation of glowing metallic life –
Nothing remains of vision.

Love still a prisoner –
              vain conception
Or a cheap thrill sold on credit.
   A commotion pouring in torrents,
   This unmanned flock is all yours.

PAST

Time is of no essence here
Could be day or night,
A fag with hair of smoke
Undresses near a memory.

A short old man,
Who laughs and cries,
Has just caught a little fish
To present me with, wretch that I am.

But why does the old man appear
To have no home to live in?
The sky, the gypsy's ceiling,
Is always alluring to him.

Ես կանչում եմ, որ գա ներս՝
Նա գլուխն է օրորում,
Եվ սուզվում է ձկան պես
Աներևույթ ջրերում։

ԱՆԱՊԱՏ

Լռությամբ իր վայրի
Դժո՞խք է, թե՞ եղեմ
Անապատն ամայի,
Որ փռվել է իմ դեմ։

Ղողանջս չի հյուսվում
Փրկության երազին,
Հնչյուններն են քավում
Շիկացած ավազին։

Ես խաղաղ երգում եմ՝
Հայացքս երկնքին,
Ինձ դանդաղ լքում է
Արևքամ իմ հոգին։

Հրեղեն մի գունդ է
Բիբերիս մոխրանում։
Ու հեծո անդունդն է
Անընդհատ խորանում։

ԳԻՇԵՐԱՅԻՆ ԷՍՔԻԶ

Ոչ մի հնչյուն չգնցաց,
Ոչ ոք չասաց՝ ներս արի –
Գիշերը լույս էր հանցած
Ու լռություն էր վայրի։

I ask him to come inside
But he shakes his head,
Disappearing like a fish
In the depths of invisible waters.

DESERT

Is it hell or Eden
The bare desert
Spread before me
With its savage silence?

My chimes don't blend
With dreams of salvation,
The notes are
Smeared over the molten sand.

I sing calmly,
My eyes lifted skywards,
My soul, bled to death,
Leaves me with ease.

A blazing sphere
Turns to ashes on my pupils,
And then the chasm
Gets deeper and deeper.

NOCTURNAL SKETCH

Not a single note to hear
No one ever said *come in* –
That night a light disappeared
And a savage silent din.

Վերից իջնող մի փաք կայծ
Գոնե երազ արարի,
Որ պապկերն այս լռակյաց
Տեսիլքներով զարդարի:

Երկնքի մեջ մի հարրած՝
Հանճարների պես բարի՝
Սլանում է հոգին բաց
Անդունդները խավարի:

Ոչ մի հնչյուն չգնգաց,
Ոչ ոք չասաց՝ ներս արի –
Գիշերը երգ էր հանգած
Ու լռություն էր վայրի:

* * *

Խեղճ ու կրակ մի մոմ
Անձայր խավարի մեջ
Փոքրիկ մի անկյուն էր
Լուսավորել,
Գինով քամիները
Եկան հոհռալով
Եվ փորձեցին նրա
Խինդը մարել,
Բայց երկարեց բոցը՝
Թրթռաց ու պարեց
Եվ ավելի դարձավ
Լուսափրփուր –
Մեր հոգու մեջ վառվող
Պայծառ մի մասնիկ կա,
Որ չի թողնում լինենք
Կապարյալ կույր:

May a fierce spark from above
At least bring about a dream
To adorn this image dumb
With the visions never seen.

Now a drunkard in the sky
Soars with an open soul
To the gorges of the dark
Like the kind genius we know.

Not a single chime to hear
No one ever said *come in* –
That night a song disappeared
And a savage silent din.

***

A meagre lone candle
Had brightened
A small corner
In the infinite darkness.
Drunken winds
Guffawed
Trying to extinguish
Its joy.
But the flame stretched,
It flickered and danced
And became more
Alive with light –
A bright particle
Burning in our soul
Saves us from
Being totally blind.

* * *

Մեզ որոնեցի ալիքների մեջ՝
Իրահարսերի կապույտ վրանում,
և մինչև հիմա անխոս կարոտով
Չկներն ին խաչն են ծովից ծով փանում:
Նրանց զանգի մեջ իմ անունը կա,
Իմ անունը կա՝ չքնաղ պատկերով,
Այնտեղ ծփում է հավատը հոգու
Եվ Քրիստոսի հայացքը փիրող:

Եվ թևուկներն են փայլպլում արծաթ՝
Որպես կարոտի անբառ վերծանում,
Երգեր են սուզվում ալիքների մեջ
Եվ ալիքների թափը կորձանում:
Բայց վրանները դատարկ են այնտեղ,
Մամին փչում է շեփորը ցավի,
Եվ արցունքները շրերին թափվող
Դանդաղ իջնում են հապտակը ծովի:

ՎԻՐԱՎՈՐ ԽԱՉ

Քամելեոնների առատությունից
      խառնաշփոթ են գույներն աշխարհի,
Զույալ ծայների եղեռն է հիմա,
      եւ կոկորդներն են լցված արյունով,
Բզկտված, նեխած համբերությունս
      ո՞մ ուղեղի հետ պիտի նժարվի,
Երբ վզիպության կիկլոպների հետ
      ինձ կանգնեցրել են նույն ճանապարհին:

Ջարհուրելի է, երբ ճանաչել ես փորձում ինքդ քեզ
Նմանվում ես սարդոստայնի մեջ ընկած մժեղի,
Եվ Որի կապանքից նրա փախուստի ուղին միայնակ
Անցնում է մահվան սովից ցամաքած կոկորդի միջով:
Մինչդեռ եղել է, որ Եզոպոսի հարբած փիրոշ պես
Կարծում էի, թե ծովը կարող եմ խմել մի շնչով:
Հիմա ամեն ինչ դարձել է ունայն ու անմատչելի,

* * *

I searched for you in the waves
In the blue tent of mermaids,
And the fish still carry my cross
From sea to sea, mute with pain.
My name remains in their sculls,
My name, with an enchanting picture,
There the faith of the soul billows,
And the all-powerful gaze of the Saviour.

And their silver scales sparkle
Like the wordless rendition of loss,
Songs sink into the waves
Breaking the pace of their movement.
But the tents are empty there
As the winds on pain's trumpet blow
And tears falling on the waters
To the sea bed slowly flow.

A WOUNDED CROSS

From the abundance of chameleons
    The colours of the world are in chaos,
There's a massacre of pure voices
    And throats are choking with blood.
With whose brain should
    My torn, rotten patience be measured,
When I've been set
    on the same path as the Cyclops of folly?

Horror is when you try to know yourself
Ending up a midge tangled in a cobweb,
Whose only chance of escape passes through
A throat, dry with death's desire.
Yet there was a time when, like Aesop's drunken lord,
I too felt able to drink up the sea in one gulp.
Now everything's void, unreachable,
Dreams only harness what's real,

Եվ երազները ճշմարտությունն են կաշկանդում միայն,
Եվ զուր թվում է, թե չթառամող ծաղիկների շուրջ
Ամեն առավոտ նույն թիթեռներն են ցնծությամբ պարում:

Եվ չհասկացա՝ ամայացե՞լ է շուրջս ամեն ինչ,
Թե՞ լույսով պարված ինքս եմ հասել դուռն անապատի,
Ուր առաջնորդի կերպարանք առած՝ փանում է քամին,
Եվ վերադարձի ուղնահետքերն է ավազը խլել:
Ծարավի փենջը հոգիս մեկնում է մանկության առաջ՝
Ուր գարնան ծաղկած հմայքների շուրջ չուրն է ծիծաղում:
        Իսկ անապատի հիշողության մեջ
            վերջին անձրևն է շարունակ մաղում...
Հոգնած աչքերիս չի փեսիյանում պապկերն ուրիշի,
Թեև լավ գիտեմ, որ անապատի ավազին փռված
Փառավոր մի էգ՝ հաշիշով օծված մշուշ կփոքեր՝
Տառապած սերը գոհելով փոշոտ կրքերի առաջ,
Եվ գիտեմ նաև, որ զմայլանքի սահմաններից դուրս՝
Կուրրված սրտով հանգիստ են քայլում փշերի վրա:

Ես համբանում եմ ու ոչինչ չունեմ ձեզ հետպ կիսելու՝
Մոռթված արգանդից
        վաղածի՛ն մի լաճ
                պապիս անունից,
Քանզի Լեռը, որ հոգուս խոյանքն էր աշխարհին պարզել՝
Նահատակների բյուր ոկորների պապկեր է թվում,
Եվ ծաղիկներս չեն հասնում նրա խնկահոտ լանջին,
Միայն ճերմակող կարոտներս են կապտարին փռվում:
    – Ո՜, եղիցի լույս,
        եղիցի դրախտ,
            ու կյանք եղիցի, –
Ասում եմ, սակայն կյանքս մարում է փաք ավազներին,
Եվ հրեշտակը հավատարմության փարս է հորինում՝
Ինձ աղերսելով, որ իմ մեղավոր մարմինը լքեմ
Հանուն երկնային անթափանց լույսի ու արքայության:
    Ես Հիսուսը չեմ, ինձ շապ մի՛ սիրիր,
        Տե՜ր, շփոթում ես քո զավակներին...
Եվ խավարամերձ պապվիրանները քո նվիրյալի
Թեև իմ ներսից սիրո, բարության անուրջներ քամեց,
Բայց ես չմարեց շուրջս թափառող հուրը չարության.
Եվ հիմա նորից արյուն է թափվում խաչից վիրավոր:

And it's pointless to expect each morning
That around the everlasting flowers
The same butterflies will dance with joy.

I couldn't tell: had everything disappeared all around
Or, enchanted with the light, was I the one standing at the
                                      threshold of the desert
Where the wind always guides you disguised as leader,
And the footprints of return are devoured by the sand?
Thirst's desire spreads my soul before my childhood
Where water giggles around the blossoming delights of spring.
    And in the memories of the desert
    The last rain still falls...
Another's image won't appear before my weary eyes
Though I know full well that, lying on the sands of the desert,
A great "she" would spread a mist scented with hashish
Slaughtering her tortured love before dusty passions,
And I know as well that beyond borders of enchantment
Walking on thorns with a broken heart is easy.

I am losing my speech and have nothing to share with you
A premature lad
    from a slaughtered womb
    bearing grandfather's name,
For the mountain which stretched the flight of my soul out to the world
Seems to be an image of the countless bones of martyrs,
And my flowers can't reach its incense-perfumed slopes
Only the longings of age scatter over its peak.
    – Oh, let there be light
    and paradise
    Let there be life, –
I say, yet my life ebbs away on the scorching sand
And the angel invents a farce of loyalty
Imploring me to leave my sinful frame
For the heavenly kingdom and impenetrable light.
    I am not Jesus, don't love me too much,
    Lord, you have confused your sons
And though the enlightening commandments of your prophet
Squeezed visions of love and kindness from me,
It nonetheless couldn't put out the fire of evil wandering around
And now blood is dripping from the wounded cross again.

Տե՛ր, ուքերիդ փակ զվարթ գոհում եմ երզն այս դիվահար,
Որ գալարվում էր փիեզերական լաբիրինթոսում,
Այս քասի մեջ դեռ չեմ ընկալել գոյությունը Քո,
Արարումների առեղծվածի դեմ կույր եմ փակավին.
Եվ անզորության ադերսն է, որ իմ ձեռքն է մեկնում Քեզ՝
Այս համասփյուռ արքայությունը Քեզ շնորհելով:
Վիրավոր խաչից արյուն է թափվում աշխարհի վրա,
Եվ հոգեվարքի ափին է հասնում խիղճը մարդկային.
Որոնում է նաեւ սակայն, ավա՜ղ, չի գտնում Նոյին
Եվ ամենքին է իր ջրհեղեղյան բոթը 22նջում.
           – Այս անգամ արդեն
       Խաչի՛ արյունով հեղեղ կլինի,
       Եթե մնում եք դահճի պես կանգնած արեգակի դեմ
       Եվ թույն եք լցնում սրբազան Լեռան ամեռ կարոտին:

Lord, I sacrifice before you with joy these possessed words
Which were rolling in the labyrinth of the universe,
I haven't grasped your existence in this chaos yet.
I remain blind before the mystery of creation
And the cry of desperation stretches my hand out towards you,
Presenting this vast kingdom to you.
Blood is dripping onto the world from the wounded cross,
And human conscience reaches the realm of death,
It searches but, alas, can't find Noah,
And whispers its tidings of the flood to all –
> *This time*
> *There will be a flood of blood from the cross*
> *If you keep standing as murderers against the sun,*
> *Pouring venom over the everlasting longing of the Holy Mount.*

AZNIV SAHAKYAN

AZNIV SAHAKYAN was born in 1959 in Yerevan and studied philology at Yerevan State University. Her first poem was published in 1986 in *Literary Weekly* since when she has been published regularly in the literary press, including in the *Garoun* and *Nork* journals. She has been a member of the Writers' Union of Armenia since 1995.

She has published four collections of poetry: *Back Door* (2011), *Communion Wafer* (2001), *Respiration* (1996) and *Meteorite* (1990). Her poems have been translated into English and Swedish.

* * *

Գարունը ձայրից ձայր
Կապույտի փրոփյուն է,
Մոփեցող մի բույր
Թեթթիկ է թափում
Վարդագույն փեղ-փեղ:
Ծառը շոյված է օդով,
Հողը օծված է...
Ջուրը թիավարում է մտքում,
Լույսը՝ ջրի մեջ,
Գրկելու շարժումը
Շշուկ է երկար...
Տողը եկավ՝
Պղդավորված եմ էլի,
Ու երկինք կա վրաս,
Ձեռքեր, ճյուղեր կան մինչև ինձ հասած:
Օրը պաշարված է ցնծությամբ,
Սիրտս՝ գույներով,
Կյանքը խմվում է քսանչորս ժամ:
Գարուն է...

* * *

Երգում են ծաղիկները,
Ծառերը ոփնաթաթերին կանգնած,
Ու հիմա, երբ հասել եմ գձին երազելու,
Ջուրը բարձրանում, լվանում է մեղքերս բոլոր,
Ու սիրփս կարող է արդեն
Ճամփորդել մինչև անփեսանելին,
Ու կապույփ գույների մեջ պառկած՝
Ճերմակ եմ,
Ծլելու զգացողությամբ զարդարված:

***

Spring is pulsating blue
Everywhere,
An approaching scent
Is scattering petals
Pink, in places.
The tree is caressed by the air
The earth is sprinkled over...
Water is stirring in the mind,
Light, in the water.
The movement of writing
Is a long whisper...
The line has come,
I'm bearing fruit again
And there is sky above me,
There are hands, branches reaching out to me.
The day is besieged by joy,
My heart is full of colour,
Life can be drunk all day.
It's spring...

***

The flowers are singing,
The trees standing on tip-toes,
And now I have reached the point where I can dream,
The water rises, washing away all my sins,
And now my heart can travel
To the realm of the invisible,
And lying in blue
I am white,
Beautiful, feeling life emerging.

* * *

Սիրտս ծամում էի փափկացնելու համար:
Գիշերացողը գլորելով հասա
Ավազանի եզրին ճշմարտության
Ու հիշեցի, որ լողալ չգիտեմ...
Մնացի նվիրվածության մոլորությունը գրկած,
Ու դառնահամը ծամեց ինձ՝
Մինչեւ ինձանից բան չմնաց:

* * *

Սենյակիս անդունդը մեծանում է,
Շունչս ընկնում է բերանքսիվայր...
Ու փրկօղակը լույսի, որ միշտ ինձ մոտ եմ պահում՝
Հազցնում եմ երազներիս մեջքին,
Զգողության մեխերը
Հանում եմ իմ կողերից,
Եվ հոդին շողայկածն արդեն ես չեմ,
Լցված եմ խեցիների մեջ բանասպեղծության՝
ափ ելած,
Շնչում եմ ու շշնջում եմ անընդհատ.
«Ինձ մի՛ թող առանց քեզ, Տեր իմ»...
Օղ եմ այլեւս, լուսավոր օղ,․
Ուր արեւելքի բացումն է կայանում,
Եվ մեղուն ուշադրությանս մեջ մեղրահամն է
փարածում կյանքի,
Բզզում է երեւակայությունս,
Զարթոնքի փոշոտում է հիմա,
Փոշոտում է լռության, սպասումի:

* * *

I was chewing on my heart to soften it.
Rolling in the dew I reached
The edge of the pond of truth
And remembered I couldn't swim…
I stood holding the delusion of devotions
Then bitterness chewed on me
Until there was nothing.

* * *

The abyss in my room is growing deeper
My breath falls head first…
And I throw the life-belt of light
Which I always have to hand, to my dreams.
I remove the nails of gravity
From my sides
And I'm no longer chained to the earth,
Poured into oysters of poetry
                              upon the shore
I breathe and keep whispering,
Don't leave me, Lord…
I'm air already, luminous air,
Where the grand awakening of the East takes place
And the bee spreads the sweet taste of life.
In my consciousness
My imagination is buzzing,
It's the pollination of rebirth,
The pollination of silence, of expectations.

* * *

Կարմիր է դողը շրերի,
Աշունը թափված է ցաքուցիր,
Արեւը համ չունի,
Մերկ են բնորդները անցորդ,
Տողերը...
Մի բաժակ մշուշ կա,
Մի բաժակ հուշ,
Հեղուկ է ձայնը երկնքի,
/Ես հազար անգամ մեռա ու մնացի
Առանց քեզ/...
Անլուսանկար աշուն է՝
Իմ կրծքավանդակից ներս:

* * *

Աշունն իջնում էր
Ու մեկնվում ասֆալտին՝
Անծրելի ձայների վրա...
Պայծառ թացություն էր,
Անհունություն էր փարածման:
Մինչեւ գոտկատեղ գույների մեջ խրված՝
Թափառում էի:
Ծլարձակում էր լույսը,
Ու հափիկը բաց, ծաղիկը
Չէր փեղավորվում ծոցվոր աչքերիս մեջ:
Բովանդակությունը վարդագույնի ծածկում էր ժամանակը,
Ծահիճն էր ծածկում չգոյության...
Մի կտոր առավոտ՝ մի բերան խնձորի պես,
Մնաց կոկորդին ժամանակի:
Ամեն օրն իջնում ու փանում է ինձ
Գազաթները աշնան առասպելի...

* * *

The quiver of the water is red,
Autumn is scattered around,
The sun has no appeal,
The naked models pass by,
The words…
There is a cup of mist,
A cup of memories.
The voice of the sky is liquid,
(I died a thousand times and
ended up without you)…
Inside my ribcage
Is an un-depicted autumn.

* * *

Autumn was descending,
Stretching over the asphalt
Absorbing the sound of the rain…
There was a bright wetness,
An unbounded expansion.
I was wandering
In colours up to my waist.
Light was flashing
So my eyes couldn't take in
The seed, the flowering, of a word.
Pinkness was flooding time,
and the swamps of non-existence…
A piece of morning, like a mouthful of apples,
Was lodged in the throat of time.
Each day arrives and takes me
To the peaks of the legend of autumn…

* * *

Մութը սպվերն է ճայնիս,
Ձեռքերիս վրայով, կարոտի գնացքները մեկնում են
Ինձ գլորելով՝ աշունների ոդորաններով...
Քամին փոշի է փոում քաղաքով մեկ,
Բառերը կեսգիշերին ծարաված՝ տանջվում են։
Խճաքարերի վրա փշրվել են
Երազանքների լապտերները,
Տե՛ս, պտրվում եմ մեկ ոտքի վրա...

* * *

Խոպ է փգրուկը գիշերվա...
Քամին հող է պտրում
Եվ աղոթքներս մուրացկան։
Ես շուտ եկա միանգամից,
Ու հայելիները ծերացան...

* * *

Տերևներ՝ ուշացող անձրևների մասին խոստող,
Արև՛ ծոծրակիս նստած,
Արմավախիպ երկինք աչքերիս մեջ այրված՝ չրերով,
Հոգսի մանրէներ,
Չորեր, ձորեր, ձորեր...
Քարափներ, օգտվեք առիթից
Այսօր բառերս վերջացան...

* * *

Darkness is the shadow of my voice,
The trains of yearning set off from my hands
And roll me down the winding roads of autumns past…
The wind spreads a veil of dust all over the city.
Words are tortured with midnight thirst.
Torches of dreams
Are shattered on the pebbles.
Look! I'm twirling on one foot…

* * *

Deaf is the leech of the night…
The wind is spinning the soil
And my begging prayers.
All of a sudden, I turn around
And the mirrors have aged…

* * *

Leaves, telling of delayed rains,
Sun, resting on my neck,
Uprooted sky burnt in my watering eyes,
Microbes of trouble,
Gorges, gorges, gorges…
Rocks, this is your chance,
Today I ran out of words…

* * *

Տողերի թշունները սն
Կարմիր փերն են ուռում
Ու կարոտներ՝ դեղնած:
Ես թերթում եմ ինձ՝
Գիշերվա մեջ նստած...
Մեկն ուզում է քայլել
Իրերի վրայով սրտիս –
Հեփմահու օրեր են՝
ամրացված աչքերիս:

* * *

Ես քար եմ երեխի,
Չէ', քար եմ հասարակ,
Ու մեջս արյուն կա՝
Անիշելի ժամանակներից մնացած,
Լեզուն ադոթքով՝ ճզմված, հրեշտակներով,
Որ շշնջում են. «Մի՛ մոռացիր մեզ, մի՛ մոռացիր»...
Եվ փշրվում է աչքս՝ կարծրությունից երկնքի,
Ու մակարդվում է լեզուս,
Ու ոսկոր ավերակներ էր բլուրում սաղմոսների...
Ես քար եմ՝ կշռաքարն աշխարհի,
Ու մեջս մրմուռ կա զաղթական ուքերի...
Շքերթում են ազգավները
Նույն կոհնչով,
Ու մեր ձայնն անձայն է երկնքում նույնպես:

* * *

Բառերը լապտերներ են փնտրում
Ու ճանապարհի են խոսպանում ուրախության,
Ես բոբիկ ուքերով փորում եմ ջուրը գիշերվա,
Ու մերկ է ձայնն քեզ կանչող:

* * *

The black birds of the lines
Are eating red leaves
And golden longings.
I flip my own pages,
Sitting the night out...
Someone wishes to walk
Over the waters of my heart –
Posthumous days
Attached to my eyes.

* * *

Perhaps I am stone,
No, I truly am stone,
And there is blood in me
Left from times unknown,
Full of prayers, squeezed, with angels
Whispering *Don't forget us, don't...*
And my eye shatters from the hardness of the sky,
And my tongue clots,
And my bones pile up ruins of psalms...
I am stone, the counter-balance of the world,
I bear the soreness of exiled feet...
The crows parade
With the same croaks,
And our voices are silent even in the sky.

* * *

Words are seeking torches
And promise a path towards happiness,
With bare feet, I dig into the waters of the night,
And my voice is naked as it calls you.

* * *

Ծառերի նման, որ ծաղկում ու թափվում են սիրուն,
Առանց մտածելու, թե փառավորություն են թողնում
ուրիշների վրա,
Կանգնում եմ:
Աչքս ծակում է ժամանակը,
Խոսքերը թափվում են մաքուր,
Ամեն ինչ իմն է –
Ես սիրեցի բառերը:
Ու սարերը նոր սարեր ծնեցին,
Ծովերը՝ ծովեր,
Արեգակն արեւ, ծաղիկը՝ ծաղիկ...
Քարերը փափկեցին,
Ջուրը կոշրացավ, դարձավ երկաթ,
Ներկը՝ գույն, երազն՝ իրականություն:
Քայլեցի մի քուռ փառերը գրկած,
Որտեղ բարուր տեսա երգի խոնարհվեցի,
Հիմա բոլոր բառերը հավաքել եմ շուրջս
Արևակիր, լուսաբորբոք, մեղրաբերան, կոշտալեզու ու
հրախանձ,
Բառերը՝ շնչավոր, կենդանի, կենդանակերպ,
Մեծամասամբ՝ գիշատիչ,
Բառեր, որ կերան ինձ:

* * *

Ձևերի մեջ սրտիս
Քայլում եմ որպես մահկանացու շշուկ,
Խրվում եմ ցրտի մեջ կորստյան՝
Մինչև վերջ ու դուրս չեմ գալիս...
Օրը չգիտեմ որպեղից է սկսվում,
Ու ես մտնում, թե չեմ մտնում նրա մեջ,
Վաղն ուր պիտի գնամ
Եվ կգնամ արդյոք,
Քո քառսով եմ ընդմիշված,
Ու հետու է Աստված...

* * *

Like a tree, which blossoms and thins nicely
Without thinking that it is making an impression
on others,
I stand.
My eye pierces time,
Words fall, crystal clear,
Everything is mine –
I liked the words.
And mountains gave birth to new mountains,
The seas to seas,
The sun bore a new sun, the flower, flowers...
The stone softened,
Waters stiffened, turned into iron,
Paint turned into colour, dreams into reality.
I walked holding a handful of letters,
Bowed wherever I saw a cradle for songs.
I have now gathered all the words around me,
Sunny, bright, sweet-lipped, sharp-tongued and charred,
Words which are breathing, alive, creature-like,
Mostly predators,
Words, which have devoured me.

* * *

In the snows of my heart
I walk like a passing whisper,
I'm immersed in the chill of loss
And can't escape...
I haven't a clue where the day begins
And whether I am included in it,
Or where I should go tomorrow
And whether I should go at all.
I'm interrupted by your chaos
And God is too far away...

* * *

Լուսինն ազդագրի նման կախվեց փողոցի վրա՝
Այսպափ մոտ չէի տեսել,
Այնպես որ, սփիտված եմ ոչ ագուրվել՝ հեռու
                                        բարեկամի պես:
Հարցնում եմ. «Ո՞նց ես, ի՞նչ ես անում այս կողմերում»:
Նա թե. «Նեղում եմ նեղսրտությունը գիշերվա,
                                        խաբեությունը քնի,
Մոլորությունը վաղահաս, մենության թանձրությունը:
        Վերականգնում եմ ինքնաշիտակցությունը
                                        գոյության,
Ծղրիդների ներդաշնակ տրտվյունը՝ արյան մեջ,
Խոտերի ներկայությունը կանաչ,
Ծլելու պատրաստակամությունը՝ հավերժի խորքերում:
        Կազմակերպում եմ հանդիպում՝
                Աղբյուր-ակունքի հետ՝ ժայռից բխող, որից
                                        թույլատրվում է
Մի բուռ խմել գժվելու պայմանով...
        Ջայնային հաղորդակցություն՝ լեռների հետ,
Անձավների հետ՝ ճգնավոր:
        Ուղեւորություն դեպի մշուշ:
        Մահվան թագվորություն:
Մութք գործելուց առաջ ակնկալվում է՝
Ճաշակել բոլոր պտուղները խակ ու հասուն
                                        /ներառյալ՝ խնձորը/,
Խորհուրդ չի տրվում խոսել Տիրոջ հետ...
Կարող եք նետվել դեպի ճշգրիտ գիտությունը
                                        տառապանքի,
Չգայ բացարձակ որբությունը,
Կարող եք քայլել պարիսպների վրայով՝ նախկին
                                        քաղաքների,
Թեւավոր ձիեր կարող եք վարձել՝ ծովից ծով անցնելու
                                        համար...
Ժամանակին վայրէջք կատարելու պայմանագրով:
        Վերադառնալը պարտադիր է»:
Ես այս ամենը կարդում, հետանում եմ դանդաղ,
Ազդագիրը մեծ մնում է կախված՝ օդի մեջ գիշերվա...

* * *

The moon hung over the street like a billboard,
I had never seen her so close,
So I'm obliged to greet her like an old
                                      acquaintance.
How are you? What brings you here? I ask,
She replies, *I'm here to discard the vexation of the night,*
                               the deceit of sleep,
Premature delusions, the thickness of solitude.
    I'm here to restore the consciousness of
                                existence
The harmonious trampling of the crickets in the bloodstream,
The green presence of the grass,
Its willingness to sprout in the depths of eternity.
    I arrange meetings
        With springs born from the rocks, from which
                                you are allowed
To take a sip on condition that you'll go mad
    A voice communing with the mountains
With the hermit caves.
    A Trip to Mist.
    The Kingdom of Death.
Before entering you are expected
To have tasted all the fruit, whether ripe or not,
                                (including the apple)
It is not advised to speak to the Lord…
You can throw yourselves towards the natural science of
                                suffering,
Feel yourselves absolute orphans,
You can walk over the fortresses of bygone
                                towns,
You can hire winged horses to cross the seas…
With a contract to land on time.
        Return is compulsory.
I read all this and leave slowly,
The huge billboard remains hanging in the night air…

ANATOLI HOVHANNISYAN

PHOTO: AUTHOR'S ARCHIVE

ANATOLI HOVHANNISYAN was born in 1957 in Yerevan. He completed his studies in Philology at Yerevan State University and his work has appeared in the national press since 1981. He has published two collections of poetry – *Warm Country* (2000) and *Mirror* (2010) – and has also compiled and edited several books.

He has received numerous literary awards.

* * *

Ես ինձ փնտրում եմ
Իմ փլատակների տակ
Ու չեմ գտնում.
Այնտեղ կապույտ երկինք է...

* * *

Բանաստեղծության փողՙ
Վերքի նման մերկ,
Ես նայում եմ հայելունՙ քեզ,
Չկարողանալով փախչել
Եվ չկարողանալով չնայել...

* * *

Օրացույցի մեջ կորած մի օր,
Ճակատագրի նվերՙ
Ես անցել եմ քո կողքով
Այդպես չնկատելով փշրվում են ծաղիկը...

* * *

Քամին մոխիրը համբուրելով
Այրել է շուրթերը.
Մթության մեջ չարդված
Ավազի ժամացույցը լեզու չունի,
Եվ նրա մեռած նյարդը
Ընդամենը թել է
Քո զգեստին կպած...

* * *

I seek myself
In my own ruins
And find nothing
A blue sky is all there is...

* * *

A line of poetry
Like an open wound,
I look into the mirror, at you,
Unable to escape
Or look away...

* * *

A lost day on the calendar
A gift of fortune
I have passed you by
This is how flowers are crushed, unseen...

* * *

The wind has burnt its lips
Kissing the ashes,
The hour glass, smashed in the dark,
Has no voice,
And its dead nerve
Is a mere thread
Stuck on your dress...

* * *

Քնած ես,
Խավարում թաղվել է աշխարհը,
Արթուն եմ միայն ես՝
Պատուհանիդ լույսի նման,
Որ մոռացել ես անջատել...

* * *

Ես կորչում եմ քո նվաղ աչքերում
Ծով ներվված քարի նման,
Բառերն անվարժ, անձեռք գունդուկծիկ
Կկործ են պատռում
Ու չեն դառնում գործ։
Երկնքի անդորը կապույտը
Փլվել է վրաս,
Քո շողացող շուրթերին
Ես երանությունից հալվող փաթիլ եմ...

* * *

Ես ասպղերի արփացոլանքը
Երազում մսխած,
Գեփինը չանգռող
Շնչահատ գետ եմ...

* * *

Մենակ են ծառերը,
Եվ մենակ է
Նրանց ճղակոտոր անող
Քամին...

* * *

You are asleep
The world is buried in darkness
I am the only one awake
Like the light in your window
Which you forgot to switch off…

* * *

I am lost in your fainting eyes
Like a stone thrown into the sea,
Clumsy words, wingless, wound in a ball
Tear at the throat
Unable to become a scream.
The blue prayer of the sky
Has collapsed over me,
I am a snowflake
Melting with joy upon your glowing lips…

* * *

I'm a breathless river
Scratching the earth
Having devoured the reflection of the stars
In my dreams…

* * *

The trees are alone
And alone
Is the wind
Tearing them apart…

* * *

Դապարկությունը լցվում է վախի ճիչով։
Լարը, որի վրայով
Լուսնորդի նման անցել եմ,
Զգված է եղել ինձնից՝ քեզ,
Իսկ դու չկաս...
Արճճե մշուշը գրվում է,
Եվ առուձախի կեղծ կշեռքների
Խաղացկուն աչքերով
Սիրվա են մրնում շուկայի մազիլները։
Եմ՝ խաչի վրա ճիշս կորցրած,
Եմ՝ պարանոցիդ շղթայից պոկված խաչ՝
Խոլ ու կույրերի վազվզոցում ոտնատակ,
Եմ՝, որ էլ ձմռան սառած ապակուն փարված
Բյուրերի մեջ մի հատիկ աստղիկը չեմ,
Այլ փխեղծ գոյությունից
Հալված
Ու չզիտես ուր գլորվող
Կաթիլի մաս...

* * *

Ես եմ, ինչ ունես այս կյանքում,
Կորցրած հեռախոսահամարը
Տարիներ հետո
Սրճարանի նույն սեղանին փնտրող միամիտ,
Մերկությամբ
Երկնքի կապույտը խոցող
Վարից վեր կեղեւահան ծառ՝
Ինքդ քեզնից դուրս գալով
Դու փորձում ես հեռանալ
Ինձ թողնելով,
Ինչը քոնը չի եղել երբեք...

* * *

Emptiness is filled with screams of fear,
The tightrope, on which
I have been walking like a lunatic,
Was stretched from me to you
But you aren't there...
The leaden mist lifts
And the claws of the market pierce my heart
With the deceitful eyes
Of rigged scales of trade.
I have lost my scream on the cross,
I am the cross torn from the chain on your neck,
Crushed in the frenzy of the deaf and the blind.
No more am I the single starlet among the millions
Holding onto the winter, the frozen window pane,
But rather
A mere fraction of a drop
Melted
By the grotesque warmth
Rolling towards heaven knows where...

* * *

I am all you have in life,
Naively looking for the lost
Phone number, years later, on the same café table,
A tree stripped of bark,
Piercing the blue of the sky
With my nudity.
Tearing away from yourself
You try to walk away,
Leaving me with
What was never yours...

* * *

Ես ինքս իմ մեջ խոնված
Ուռկան եմ,
Որ Աստված նետել է ծով
Ու մոռացել...

* * *

Ես կրկնում եմ անունս
Ինքս ինձ չմոռանալու համար
Հիշողության հնացած ժապավենը
Սահում է դանդաղ
Հարազատ դեմքերը երեւում են ավելի ու ավելի աղոտ,
Տրոհվում, ձեւախեղվում է
Կապարելության պապրանքը
Եվ չորացող լճերի որբացած ափերին ջուրը
Թվում է, թե
Նոսրացած օզոնային շերտի
Արտասուքն է.
Ես կրկնում եմ անունս
Ինքս ինձ չմոռանալու համար...

* * *

Ես ապրում եմ սպասման մեջ,
Կարծես ծաղիկների գերեզմանում:
Ալիքի վրա բարձրացած
Ալիքի նման,
Գազաթ լինելու արկումով
Եվ փշրվելու խոնարհությամբ
Շունչս պահած՝
Ես համրորեն փարրալուծվել եմ
Վիճակի գգայարաններում
Եվ փորձում եմ դառնալ բաժանման գծի սպին...
Պապակ ցայտաղբյուրի եզրին
Մոռացած, թե ինչու էին եկել,
Ճնճղուկներ են հավաքվել,
Որոնց չի էլ նկատում
Ցեխաջրում չոր հացը թրջող
Աղռավը...

* * *

I'm a fishing net
All tangled up within myself,
That God threw into the sea
And forgot…

* * *

I keep repeating my name
In order not to forget myself.
The worn tape of memories
Glides along slowly,
Familiar faces fade away,
The illusion of perfection
Is split, disfigured,
And the waters on the orphaned shores of dried-up lakes
Seem to be
Tears
Of the thinning ozone layer.
I keep repeating my name
In order not to forget myself…

* * *

I live in anticipation
As if in the grave of flowers.
Like a wave
Riding on waves,
Holding my breath
With the stiffness of a mountain peak
While bowing to the inevitable,
I have mutely dissolved
In the senses of circumstances,
Trying to become a scar on the dividing line…
Some sparrows have gathered
On the edge of the fountain,
Having forgotten why they came.
The crow, dunking its dry bread in the muddy waters,
Doesn't even notice them.

* * *

Մենակ եմ
Անհուսության կողը խրվող,
Ճառագայթի նման։
Այս աշխարհը՝ մեղքի կծիկ,
Որպեղ դրախտ տանող ճանապարհը
Ամենադժորկն է թվում՝ հեշտ պատկերանալի,
Դժոխքը մնացած մասը,
Ես փնտրում ու չեմ գտնում ինձ։
Տնքոցի թափերականացված շեշտը
Ընդհանուր ոչինչ չունի
Սպասման բավիղներում խարխափող
Չհնչած հեռախոսազանգի
Վերջին շնչի հետ.
Գտնվածը փողպղարձն է
Ես՝ գծիկով երկատված
Բառ...

* * *

Գեղանկարի պատառոտված կտորներ՝
Երազ.
Ես հսկա փաթալված – կտրտված ծառ եմ
Ճերմակ, կուրացնող բնով,
Հարեանող հատվածների
Անհասկանալի ինքնությամբ։
Անտեր մնացած ստվերն՝
Ապաստարան մեռած թռչունների,
Իրականը միայն դեսուդեն սիրող հայացքս է
Այս աշխարհում
Հարբած ամպի նման
Իր ամբողջությունը փնտրող...

* * *

I am alone
Like a shaft of light,
Piercing the side of hopelessness.
This world is a jumble of sins
Where the road to heaven
Seems the smoothest, the easiest, to imagine
And hell is what remains,
I seek and can't find myself.
The theatricality of a moan
Has nothing in common
With the last breath
Of the unmade phone call
Groping in the labyrinth of anticipation.
What's found is the carried-over syllable…
I am a word
bisected by a hyphen…

* * *

Torn pieces of a painting
A dream –
I am a huge, fallen, mutilated tree
With a blindingly white trunk
And an unidentifiable jumble of pieces,
My orphaned shadow
A shelter for dead birds.
The only reality in this world
Is my wandering gaze
Like a wasted cloud
Looking for its substance…

* * *

Փոշի,
Ծաքծկված աչքերով հող՝
Հայացքիս անդրադարձը
Ոչնչի չսպասող անդորրում,
Լքված, իրացվող փների հորանջող գոյություն՝
Արմատախիլ ծառեր՝
Ազդավներ, ազդավներ լրացումով։
Շինադրի կոպտակներից աչք ցավեցնելով
Նայում էր
Ցորենի սանդը...
Ավագի ժամացույցի անթռում
Վեր պարզած ձեռքերը դեռ երեւում են,
Եթե նորից շոջվի ժամանակը
Գուցե ես էլ ոչինչ չիիշեմ,
Դառնալով փշրված սանդ
Նոր լցված հիմքի
Բետոնե շաղախում...

* * *

Լուսումութին ձյունը՝
Ճանապարհից հոգնած՝ քնած է.
Ես նայում եմ
Կարծես օրորցի։
Ծերմակ խաղաղության նիրհում
Սուզվել են
Քաղաքն ու բոլոր հիշատակները։
Տափարակ դարձրած բլրի
Ներդաշնակության պատրանքը,
Երբ երկնքից չես նայում,
Ես եմ հորինել,
Եվ ես եմ,
Որ բյուր եմ եղել...

* * *

Dust,
Soil like cracked eyes,
The reflection of my look
In the calmness of non-expectancy,
The yawning presence of abandoned houses for sale,
Uprooted trees,
With crows, crows on top.
A pestle and mortar
Stares like a piercing eye
From a pile of building waste…
In the bulb of an hourglass
Raised hands are still visible.
If time turns again
Perhaps I too, would remember nothing,
Becoming a shattered mortar
In the concrete mix
Of some newly-laid foundations.

* * *

The snow sleeps in the twilight,
Tired from its journey,
And I seem to be looking
At a cradle.
The city and all its memories
Are submerged
In the slumber of a white peace.
I have invented
The illusion of harmony
For flattened hills,
When not observed from the sky,
And I am the one
Who was once a hill…

ԵՐԲ ՎԵՐՔԸ ԴԱՌՆՈՒՄ Է ԿՈՉՏՈՒԿ

Երբ վերքը դառնում է կոշտուկ,
Իսկ հոգին կարտոնե դատարկ տուփ,
Դու կախվում ես դիմահայաց պատերից`
Հայհոյանքի արժեք չունեցող
Ժամկետանց ազդագրերի մտրացկանությամբ...
Ահագնացող լռության ձայնը
Հեռվից նետված քար է,
Որ գալիս, գալիս, չի հասնում քեզ,
Աշխարհային գոյությունդ`
Բողոք մթնոլորտային ճնշման դեմ.
Քո մեջ վառվող մոմը լույս տալու տեղ չունի...
Մոլորված երեխայի լացի նման անսփոփ`
Ինչ-որ մեկը ներսից ծեծում է
Դուռը,
Բայց փեսնող աչքեր չկան,
Եվ դու էլ արդեն խուլ ես...

    * * *

Մայրուղուն դաշված
Հազիվ նշմարելի կենդանու մարմին,
Որին արդեն չեն նկատում ավտոմեքենաները,
Կռակ տված խոցան,
Ես գնում եմ առաջ,
Եվ հայացքս
Չգիտակցված արցունքի մշուշոտ ծովերով
Նավարկում է դեպի իր խորքը:
Կանգառը շունչ առնելու համար է,
Բայց ես դեռ չգիտեմ այդ մասին
Եվ փորձում եմ
Փակել ականջներս`
Չլսելու համար
Սրտիս պայթելու ձայնը...

WHEN THE WOUND TURNS INTO A CALLUS

When the wound turns into a callus
And your soul into an empty cardboard box,
Imploring, you hang from facing walls
Like an out-of-date billboard
Which lacks the value even of a swear word...
The increasing volume of silence
Is a stone thrown from afar
Which keeps coming but never reaches you,
Your earthly existence
A protest against atmospheric pressure,
The candle burning within has nowhere to illuminate...
From inside, someone knocks
At the door
With the helplessness of a lost child, crying,
But there are no watchful eyes
And you are already deaf...

* * *

Flattened on the motorway
An animal carcass, barely visible,
Which by now passing cars fail to notice,
Stubble on fire,
And, moving forward,
My gaze
Sails through the misty seas of unperceived tears
towards its depths.
The stop is for taking a breath
But I am not aware of it yet
And I'm trying
To close my ears
Not to hear
The explosion of my own heart...

* * *

Խառը երազների շփոթից
Ես արթնացել եմ
Ցայգուցրիվ։
Շեղբի պես սառը իրականությունը
Կիսել է ինձ ճամփաբաժնի նման։
Այս զարմանալի աշխարհի թեւին
Ես մի օր իջա
Ճերմակ աղավնու փեսքով՝
Քաղցած հայացքները
Ինձ ապաստարան թվացին,
Եվ ես, որ կապույտ երկնքի թռթիռն էի՝
Դարձա կերակուր...

* * *

I have woken
In a mess
From the confusion of my dreams,
Reality, cool as a blade,
Has split me in two like a fork in the road.
On the wings of this amazing world
I descended one day
In the form of a dove,
The hungry looks
Seeming like shelters to me
And I, the throb of blue skies,
Turned into food...

HASMIK SIMONIAN

HASMIK SIMONIAN was born in 1987 in Yerevan. She completed her studies at Yerevan State University of Pedagogy in 2008, specializing in Philology. In 2009 she completed a course in journalism at the Caucasus Institute of Journalism in Yerevan.

She has published two collections of poetry, *Lunatic Words* (2005) and *Untidy Rooms* (2010). She has received many literary awards including the 2004 *Time* award, the Slavik Chiloyan award for her first collection and the 'Little Prince' award, both in 2005, and the President's Youth award in Literature and the Special Prize at the 'The Future is Ours' Festival, both in 2006. She also received the *Gretert* journal award for rhetoric and essay writing in 2008, and for poetry in 2010.

* * *

Ճերմակ լռության սփոփանքի մեջ
արշալույսներ է հագնում մի երկինք,
որ մթության մեջ դեգերում էր եւ
ծրարվում հանկարծ նամակի նման,
որի փողերին քնել էր մի սեր,
սեր, որ ծնվել էր անձրեւից առաջ
ու մի քիչ ննջել անձրեւից հետո...

Անձրեւից առաջ գունատ փողոցով
մի պարօրինակ փդա էր վազել
ու 22նջացել ծաղկավաճառին մտքում գոռալով.
... – Ի՞նձ անձրեւ է պետք...
Խնդրում եմ, փվեք մի փունջ թարմ անձրեւ...
Ծաղկավաճառը փվել էր նրան մի փունջ քմծիծաղ՝
արհամարհանքի ժապավեններով:

... անձրեւից առաջ, անձրեւից հետո...

Ծաղկավաճառը ծնվել էր երեկ՝ անձրեւից հետո,
երբ ինչ-որ կաթիլ հասկացել էր, որ
ուզում է շնչել մի քիչ թրջված օդ,
խոսել այդ մի քիչ թրջված բառերով,
որ կաթիլի պես պարփեր առաջ
արցունք էր դարձել ծանոթ փողի մեջ՝
համբուրելով թաց շուրթերը բառի...

Անձրեւից առաջ կաթիլի պես նուրբ
          մի ծաղկավաճառ
նամակ ստացավ՝ ջնջված անունով...
... ու ամեն անգամ անձրեւից առաջ
մի պարօրինակ փդա էր գալիս
          ու խնդրում անձրեւ...
... եւ դանդաղ հալվող ադմուկի միջից վերջալույսների
փողկապ էր կապում մի երիփասարդ
          Երկինք անունով,
որը քիչ առաջ հայելու դիմաց
ջնջացել էր ծանոթ մեկի պես.
... – Գիփե՞ն ինչ, փոքրիկ, երբ դու ծնվեցիր,
          անձրեւ էր գալիս...

* * *

In the solace of a white silence
dawn clothes the sky,
wandering through darkness
folded over like a letter
on the pages of which sleeps love,
love, born before the rain,
dozing after it...

before the rain a strange boy
ran through the brightening street
and – inwardly screaming – whispered to the flower girl
I need some rain...
please give me a bunch of fresh rain...
the flower girl gave him a bunch of chuckles
tied up with ribbons of scorn

... before the rain, after the rain...

the flower girl was born after the rain,
when a raindrop felt like
breathing wet air,
speaking wet words,
like a drop many years ago
turning into a familiar tear,
kissing the wet lips of a word...

before the rain the flower girl, delicate as a raindrop,
received a letter from a faded name...
... and always before the rain
a strange boy would come
       to ask for some rain...
and, through the melting noises of dusk
some youth by the name of Sky
wearing a tie,
by the mirror
had earlier whispered, as if he knew you,
You know, little one, it was raining
       when you were born.

բարև

... թվում է՝ մենք երկուսով ենք կանգնել
ժամանակի մեջ ու... սենյակում,
որտեղ ամեն ինչ թափանցիկ է, անգամ
հայելու շուրթերը, ես կանաչ եմ...
քո ժպիտը մի քիչ բեկբեկուն ու...
ինձ նմանները ավելի շուտ են ապրել ու հիմա չկան.
դու ինձ նման ես... ու ինձանից հետո ես ծնվել,
իսկ ավելի շուտ ծնվածները
չափից դուրս շատ են հավատում, որ
ամեն ինչ սահմանելի է եւ անլուծելի...
ես ափում եմ դռները... կիսաբաց աչքերով...
ու կիպրոնի ծառը, որ հեռվից մանկության
կիսաթթու բույրով է խոսում,
միայնակ է թվում...
նա լքված է իր մարմնից... ու ես
հեռանում եմ սենյակից, որտեղ թողեցի մարմինս...
... ես հիմա կիպրոնի ծառի նման
            կարոտում եմ նրան...
սենյակի դռների փոխարեն պատեր են՝
չափից դուրս ամուր,
չափից դուրս շոշափելի,
ու ես հաճախ եմ
ներողություն խնդրում մտքում՝ չհավատալով
իմ ու դիմացինիս գոյությանը...
... թվում է՝ մենք երկուսով ենք միայն
ու չափից դուրս է ամեն ինչ...
որովհետեւ
շատ տարիներ առաջ ցամաքել են հիշողությունները
ձեռացած մատների նման...
ծիծաղող հեռախոսի դողացող ձայնի պես...
ես միայնակ եմ, ու հեռախոսը, որի մյուս ծայրում
դու ես, չի խոսում ինձ հետ...
առանց նրա մենակությունը կիպրոնի
ցնորված հեքիաթ է հիշեցնում,
որ սպեղծվեց ինքնիրեն ժամանակի ընթացքում...

Գուցե ինձ թվում է, բայց մենք ընդամենը
երկուսով ենք կանգնած գնացքում
(սպվերները չեն նստում), ու քամին,
որ քեզանից չի պոկվում, ինձանից
ավելին է պահանջում... քամին...

HELLO

… it seems the two of us
are standing in time and… in a room,
where everything is transparent, even
the gape of the mirror, I'm green…
your smile, slightly refracted and…
the likes of me have lived before and are no more
you are like me… and were born after me
but those born earlier believe in too much,
in the definitiveness and insolubility of everything…
I hate doors… with their half-opened eyes…
and the lemon tree, which speaks
with the slightly sour scent
of childhood
seems lonely…
abandoned by its body… and I
am leaving the room where I left my body…
I miss it now
like the lemon tree…

there are walls instead of doors in the room
extremely solid,
extremely tangible,
and in my mind
I often apologize, sceptical
of my existence and of his, facing me…
it seems we are alone, the two of us
and everything is at the extremes
because
long ago memories dried up
like old fingers…
like the sound of a cackling phone when
I'm alone and the phone, with you at the
other end, won't talk to me…
without it, solitude seems like
the crazy tale of a lemon
that has created itself in time…

Perhaps it's my imagination, but we are
standing alone in the train
(shadows do not sit) and the wind,
which can't tear itself away from you, expects
more from me… the wind…

ճայները դանդաղ մահանում են, ավելի
դանդաղ՝ ծնվում,
ես փակ սենյակում եմ, բանալին կորցրեցիր,
այստեղ պատուհանը երկնքում է,
պապերը մարդիկ են...
ես նրանց սիրվերն եմ...
... դու քեզ մոռացել ես ժամանակից դուրս,
իսկ ես շշում եմ եմ առանց քո ներկայության ու
թեեւ թվում է, թե մենք երկուսով ենք,
ժամանակը փակում է աչքերը
կրծած եղունգները չտեսնելու համար...
հայելու թափանցիկ շուրթերը քամին
ներկում է թույլ շնչառությամբ ու թվում է՝
ես կանաչ եմ ժպտում, իսկ քո ժպիտը
բեկբեկուն է քիչ ու ինքնավստահ...
ես ու կիպրոնի մահացող ծառը սպասում ենք քեզ...
ժամանակը դեռ շշում է կամաց...
ծառը ապրում է...
– Բարեւ, շուշաց՜ա...

       * * *

Օրերը ծիսախտներ էին ծիսում,
ու փողոցների մոխրամաններում կուտակվում էին
դժգոհության քաղցած մոխիրները...
... խաղողի մերկացած ողկույզը
լվանում էր քաղցրացած
մատները.
թրշված սրբիչները մրսում էին
սեղաններին ու հանճախ բողոքում
թոքերից։
Օրերը ծիսախտներ էին ծիսում
ու որպեսզի հանույքը չավարտվեր,
մատներով ծածկում էին
գրքի վերջին երկու բառերը,
ափսոս, աչքերը կնոշ նման
նախապես գիտեին ամեն ինչ...
Օրերը ծիսախտներ էին ծիսում, ու

voices die slowly,
they are born even more slowly
I'm locked up in a room, you have lost the key,
the window here is the sky,
                      the walls are people...
I'm their shadow...
... you have forgotten yourself outside of time,
and I breathe without your presence and
though it seems there are the two of us,
time is closing its eyes
so as not to glimpse its bitten nails...
the wind colours the gape of the mirror
with a faint breath and it seems
I smile a green smile, and your smile
is slightly refracted and confident...
the dying lemon tree and I are waiting for you
time is still breathing weakly...
the tree lives...
– *Hello, I'm not late, am I?*

    * * *

Days were smoking cigarettes
and the hungry ash of discontent
was gathering in the ashtrays of the streets...
the bare bunch of grapes
was washing its sweetened
fingers,
the wet towels were freezing
on the tables and complaining
about their lungs.
The days were smoking cigarettes
and hiding the two last words of the book
with their fingers
to make the enjoyment last.
Alas, the eyes knew everything
beforehand, like a woman...
days were smoking cigarettes and

ծուխը խաղողի որթի պես
բարձրանում էր լուսարձակներով,
եւ լույսը՝ կանաչ կամ սեւ աչքերով,
կնոջ նման նախապես
գիտեր ամեն ինչ...

մերրիին

ոտքերը ասֆալտին խփում են թմբուկների նման
եռացրած մեղրի պես ջազն իջնում է շեփորի կոկորդով
հազում ես
 շարֆդ բարակ է, փաբադդ մաշված
ծխիր ինձ, խնդրում ես, ծխիր
ինչպես գիշերամիգությունն է ծխում մարմինս
ինչպես ծնողներս են ծխում մանկությունս ու դրանից հետո
ինչպես սերերս են լքում կոպտությունս ու ծխում լեզուս
ծխիր ինձ, խնդրում եմ ծխիր

ես կմռռանամ ինձնից ձնված փդաներին
եւ ոչ ոք չի համբուրի ինձ փոն մտնելուն պես եւ գնալուց առաջ չի ասի
հաջող

մահը մոտ է քիմքիս
ամենադառը շոկոլադի նման
հալված
թանձր
սեւ

գնացին բոլորը գնացին
փակում եմ աչքերս
բացում
մենք վաղուց չենք խոսում իրար հետ
եւ օրերի թմրանյութը կապվում է մեր երակներում

աղջիկս, երբ մեռնես
ես քաղաքի պոռնիկը կդառնամ
անվեր շները կքրքրեն սիրտս
եւ հեծանվորդները իմ նյարդալարերի վրայով կբարձրանան
լուսին
կիջնեն ցած

the smoke was climbing up lamp posts
like vines
and the light, like a green- or black-eyed woman
knew everything beforehand.

TO MARY

there are feet stamping on the asphalt like drums
jazz goes down the throat of a trumpet like boiled honey
you cough
your scarf is thin, your trousers worn out
smoke me, you beg, smoke
just as wetting the bed smokes my body,
just as my parents smoke my childhood and that which follows,
just as my loves abandon my harshness and smoke my tongue,
smoke me, I beg you to smoke

I shall forget the boys born to me
and no one will kiss me as I get home or say *good luck* as I leave

the closeness of death is on my pallet
like the bitterest of chocolates
melted
thick
black

they have left, they have all left
I close my eyes
open them
it's been ages since we were on speaking terms
and the day's dope turns blue in our veins

when you die, my daughter,
I'll become the whore of the town
stray dogs will savage my heart
and cyclists will ride along my nerves up to the moon
and down again

ուզում եմ փակել դուռը, բանալին կուլ տալ
չի ստացվում
ուզում եմ ժպտալ առաջվա պես
նույնը չի
ուզում գալ քեզ մոտ պեղքական իրի տեսքով
էլեկտրական կիթառի պես, մլորորակի, գրքի
ծափի փոր
աղջիկս
ծափի փոր
սիրտս ցավում է
դահլիճը դատարկ
ով կունենա քեզ համար երեխաներ աղջիկս
ով կասի նուրբ բառեր կշոյի ուսդ
ու ականջի բլթակը կկծես
կերգես անձրևի տակ
կգրես բառեր
ուտքերդ պինդ կլինեն ազդրերդ ձիգ
կասպրես էլեկտրական կիթառի մեջ
կնսպես մոլորակդ կգնաս հեռու

գիշերվա հազարին կգարթնեմ սարսափած
կոպերս ծանը կլինեն, կասպարէ
անկողինս թաց կողողդա ինձ հետո
երևի կբրացեմ աչքերս
կծխեմ
երևի կփակեմ աչքերս
ոչ ոք չի լինի կողքիս, ոչ ոք չի լինի
ցավի սուր հովրը միայն
որ գազի պես կտարածվի օդում
հանգցրած ծխախոտի նման

կգռռամ անունդ
չես լսի
կգռռամ անունդ
չես լսի
կգռռամ
կամացուկ
որ չգարթնես հանկարծ
կիթառի նյարդերի տակ քնած իմ լարային աղջիկ
խաղաղ ինչպես ոռքը ևւ ջագի պես ձեր

I want to lock the door and swallow the key
can't manage
I want to smile as before
It's not the same
I want to come to you as a useful item
like an electric guitar, a planet, a book,
clap
my child,
clap
my heart aches
the hall is empty
who will bear children for you, my daughter?
who will utter fine words, caress your shoulder?
whose earlobe will you bite?
sing in the rain
write words
your feet will be strong, your thighs firm,
you will live inside the electric guitar
ride away on your planet

I'll wake up in the middle of the night
my eyelids heavy as lead
my wet bed will shiver with me
perhaps I'll open my eyes
I'll smoke
perhaps I'll close my eyes
there will be no-one by my side, there will be no-one
only the strong smell of pain
which will scatter in the air like jazz
like an extinguished cigarette

I'll call out your name
you won't hear
I'll call out your name
you won't hear
I'll call out
quietly
so you won't wake up
my string girl sleeping under the nerves of the guitar
calm as rock and old as jazz

լսում ես, ուռքերը ասֆալտին խփում են թմբուկների նման
եթե անգամ նվագել չիմանայի
ես կվերցնեի շեփորն ո կպապմեի քեզ մի փիսուր օրորոցային
կիսավերակ մարդկանց մասին, որոնց քանդելու են վաղը
ու սարքեն նոր պոդովպա
լսում ես, ուռքերը ասֆալտին խփում են թմբուկների նման

           * * *

ակորդեոնի պես բացվող-փակվող աշունների միջից
ես գտա իմը
մազերը թռչվեցին անձրեիից
իսկ պարտությունից ձյան հոտ էր գալիս

ես աղոթում էի ձեռքերս գրպաններր դրած
քայլ առ քայլ
աշունը հեռանում էր կանգառից
անձրեի չոր հագը
կոկորդովս կուլ չէր գնում ու լացը ինչ-որ չէր սպացվում...

հուսահատությունը փորձում էր գրկել ուսերս
ես նայում էի հեռուն ու ոչինչ չէի փեսնում
քայլ առ քայլ
քայլ առ քայլ
քայլ առ քայլ

բացվող-փակվող ակորդեոն ու աշուն

փողոցներով
անիմաստ մարդիկ քայլում էին չորացած նոպաների վրայով
երեխի չգիտեին որ մազերը թռչվել էին անձրեիից
երեխի չգիտեին որ պարտությունիցս ձյան հոտ էր գալիս
երեխի չգիտեին որ հեռվում մոլորակներ կան
եւ աշնան հոտով եղաննակներ
եւ անփարբեր փողոցներ
որտեղ թավատում են բանասպեղծ-աղջիկները
եւ նրանց եպեիից փող առ փող ադկվում են փերեններր
եւ անփութի ակորդեոններր ձգվում են փողոցից փողող

can you hear it? there are feet stamping on the asphalt like drums
even if I couldn't play
I would take the trumpet and play you a sad lullaby
about shabby people, whom they will tear down tomorrow
to build a new road
can you hear it? there are feet stamping on the asphalt like drums

* * *

among autumns which stretched and squeezed like an accordion
I found my own
my hair was wet from the rain
and my defeat smelt of snow

I was praying with my hands in my pockets
step by step
autumn was receding from the bus-stop
the dry cough of the rain
couldn't be swallowed and the tears somehow wouldn't come…

hopelessness tried to embrace my shoulders
I was looking into the distance but could see nothing
step by step
step by step
step by step

a stetching-squeezing accordion and autumn

in the streets
people walked senselessly on dry notes
perhaps unaware that my hair was wet from the rain
perhaps unaware that my defeat smelt of snow
perhaps unaware that there are planets far away
and seasons smelling of autumn
and world-weary streets
where poet-girls wander
and behind them line by line the leaves fall off
and caseless accordions stretch from street to street

ցնցուդից վրաք շիթով իջնում են անձրևները
եւ ծույորեն մեռնոդ մափները բարձրանում են թռչունների պես
քայլ առ քայլ
քայլ առ քայլ
քայլ առ քայլ...

երկիր մոլորակի ամենասովորական եկեղեցիներից մեկում
ես ասպծուն ներկայանում էի ամենափխուր ադոթքով
եւ նոր սանրվածքով
(որը փուն մտնելուց առաջ վերջնականապես կորձանվելու էր)
դիմացի աղջիկը սրբում էր քիթը
ինձանից առաջ երկու հոգի որոշել էին բոլոր մոմերը գնել
ես ձեռքերս դրել էի գրպանս
եւ զանգի էի սպասում...
քայլ առ քայլ
քայլ առ քայլ
քայլ...

and rains fall in warm torrents from the shower
and the lazily dying fingers take off like birds
step by step
step by step
step by step

in a most ordinary church on planet earth
I appeared before God with the saddest of prayers
and a new hair-do
(which would be completely ruined before I reached home)
the girl in front was wiping her nose
the people ahead decided to buy all the candles
I had my hands in my pockets
waiting for a chime…
step by step
step by step
step…

ABOUT THE TRANSLATOR & EDITOR / 125

RAZMIK DAVOYAN was born in 1940 in Mets Parni, Spitak, Armenia. At the age of nine he moved to Leninakan with his family where he graduated from the local Medical College in 1958. In 1959 he moved to Yerevan to study Philology and History at the State Pedagogic University and graduated in 1964. During his student years he worked as proof reader for the *Literary Weekly* and as a member of the founding editorial board of *Science and Technology* monthly, editing the Life Sciences and Medical sections. From 1965 to 1970 he was editor of the poetry and prose section of the *Literary Weekly*. From 1970 to 1975 he worked as senior adviser at the Committee for Cultural Relations with the Diaspora. From 1975 to 1990 he worked as Secretary of the Central Committee for Armenia's State Prizes. In 1989 he was appointed Deputy Chairman of the Parliamentary Commission for the Earthquake Struck Disaster Area. In 1994 he became the first elected president of the Writers' Union of Armenia. From 1999 to 2003 he served as Adviser (on cultural and educational issues) to the President of the Republic of Armenia. From 2004 to date he is Adviser to the Director of the Armenian Public TV.

His first poem was published in 1957 in the Leninakan *Daily Worker*. Since then he has published well over thirty volumes in Armenian as well as in Russian, Czech and English translation. His works were widely translated all over the former Soviet Union and published in innumerable literary magazines and journals. Selections of poems have also been translated and published in literary periodicals in Italy, France, Syria, former Yugoslavia, Iran, China and the USA. His children's poetry book *Winter Snowflake, Spring Blossom*, published in Russian translation in 1980, sold four hundred and fifty thousand copies in only two weeks all over the former Soviet Union.

In 1971 Davoyan received Armenia's Youth Organization Central Committee Prize for Literature. In 1986 he received Armenia's State Prize for Literature. In 1997 he received the Order of St. Mesrop Mashtots from the President of Armenia for his achievements and services to the country. In 2003 he received the President's Prize for Literature for his children's book *Little Bird at the Exhibition* and in 2012, he was awarded the prestigious Commonwealth of Independent States Interstate Prize.

Three of his significant books were blocked from publication by the Soviet regime. *Requiem* was blocked for five years before it was published in Yerevan in 1969. *Massacre of the Crosses* was also blocked and was first published in Beirut in 1972. *Toros Rosslin* was also first published in New York in 1984 because of the block on its publication in Soviet Armenia.

Razmik Davoyan lives in Yerevan, Armenia.

Born in Tehran of Armenian parents, ARMINÉ TAMRAZIAN was educated in three languages (Armenian, Farsi and English). After receiving her BA degree in English in Tehran, she went on to study Linguistics at University College, London University, where she completed her MA and PhD degrees. She has published three volumes of literary translations and worked as lecturer at Yerevan State University and Yerevan State "Brusov" University for Linguistic Studies. She has also carried out research as a visiting scholar at the University of Toronto.

Classical music is also an important part of her life. She has studied the piano from a very young age and given many performances as an amateur pianist. Having sung in a children's and youth choir from the age of five, during her student years in London she became a member of the Royal Choral Society and sang in the choir for four years until she moved to Yerevan, Armenia, where she currently lives with her family.

Other anthologies of poetry in translation published
in bilingual editions by Arc Publications include:

Altered State: An Anthology of New Polish Poetry
EDS. ROD MENGHAM, TADEUSZ PIÓRO, PIOTR SZYMOR
Translated by Rod Mengham, Tadeusz Pióro *et al*

*A Fine Line: New Poetry from Eastern
& Central Europe*
EDS. JEAN BOASE-BEIER, ALEXANDRA BÜCHLER, FIONA SAMPSON
Various translators

*A Balkan Exchange:
Eight Poets from Bulgaria & Britain*
ED. W. N. HERBERT

*The Page and The Fire:
Poems by Russian Poets on Russian Poets*
ED. PETER ORAM
Selected, translated and introduced by Peter Oram

Six Slovenian Poets
ED. BRANE MOZETIČ
Translated by Ana Jelnikar, Kelly Lennox Allen
& Stephen Watts, with an introduction by Aleš Debeljak
NO. 1 IN THE 'NEW VOICES FROM EUROPE & BEYOND' ANTHOLOGY SERIES,
SERIES EDITOR: ALEXANDRA BÜCHLER

Six Basque Poets
ED. MARI JOSE OLAZIREGI
Translated by Amaia Gabantxo,
with an introduction by Mari Jose Olaziregi
NO. 2 IN THE 'NEW VOICES FROM EUROPE & BEYOND' ANTHOLOGY SERIES,
SERIES EDITOR: ALEXANDRA BÜCHLER

Six Czech Poets
ED. ALEXANDRA BÜCHLER
Translated by Alexandra Büchler, Justin Quinn
& James Naughton, with an introduction by Alexandra Büchler
NO. 3 IN THE 'NEW VOICES FROM EUROPE & BEYOND' ANTHOLOGY SERIES,
SERIES EDITOR: ALEXANDRA BÜCHLER

Six Lithuanian Poets
ED. EUGENIJUS ALIŠANKA
Various translators, with an introduction by Eugenijus Ališanka
NO. 4 IN THE 'NEW VOICES FROM EUROPE & BEYOND' ANTHOLOGY SERIES,
SERIES EDITOR: ALEXANDRA BÜCHLER

Six Polish Poets
ED. JACEK DEHNEL
Various translators, with an introduction by Jacek Dehnel
NO. 5 IN THE 'NEW VOICES FROM EUROPE & BEYOND' ANTHOLOGY SERIES,
SERIES EDITOR: ALEXANDRA BÜCHLER

Six Slovak Poets
ED. IGOR HOCHEL
Translated by John Minahane, with an introduction by Igor Hochel
NO. 6 IN THE 'NEW VOICES FROM EUROPE & BEYOND' ANTHOLOGY SERIES,
SERIES EDITOR: ALEXANDRA BÜCHLER

Six Macedonian Poets
ED. IGOR ISAKOVSKI
Various translators, with an introduction by Ana Martinoska
NO. 7 IN THE 'NEW VOICES FROM EUROPE & BEYOND' ANTHOLOGY SERIES,
SERIES EDITOR: ALEXANDRA BÜCHLER

Six Latvian Poets
ED. IEVA LEŠINSKA
Translated by Ieva Lešinska, with an introduction by Juris Kronbergs
NO. 8 IN THE 'NEW VOICES FROM EUROPE & BEYOND' ANTHOLOGY SERIES,
SERIES EDITOR: ALEXANDRA BÜCHLER

Six Catalan Poets
ED. PERE BALLART
Translated by Anna Crowe, with an introduction by Pere Ballart
NO. 9 IN THE 'NEW VOICES FROM EUROPE & BEYOND' ANTHOLOGY SERIES,
SERIES EDITOR: ALEXANDRA BÜCHLER